Book 4

An introduction to marketing

Written by Anja Schaefer

The Open University Walton Hall, Milton Keynes MK7 6AA

First published 2006. Second edition 2010. Third edition 2011.

© 2011 The Open University

Edited and designed by The Open University.

Printed and bound in the United Kingdom by Charlesworth Press, Wakefield.

ISBN 978 1 8487 3588 0

3.1

MIX
Paper from
responsible sources
FSC® C016379

Contents

Introduction to Book 4

Welcome to Book 4 of B120. This book gives an introduction to marketing theory and practice. Marketing is a highly visible and important aspect of modern business, dealing as it does with attracting and keeping customers. No commercial business could survive without customers as they are usually its only source of income: satisfying customer expectations is therefore a vital part of business management. Not-for-profit and public sector organisations must equally satisfy the users of their services in order to maintain their funding level and keep the business running.

Throughout the book, you will find a number of activities. These are designed mainly to help you relate the concepts you study to your own experience of marketing practice. Although you probably have no direct work experience of marketing, as a consumer you will have come into contact with numerous instances of marketing practice and will be able to build on this experience. Some of the activities relate to essential further readings; others ask you to look up information on the World Wide Web. (Please note that website addresses may change from time to time. If you experience problems, use a web search engine such as Google or Yahoo! to find the site in question.) You should always refer to your Study Companion to gain the most from these activities and your overall learning.

Aims and objectives

The aims of Book 4 are to:

- explain the role of marketing in a business;
- explain various aspects of marketing strategy and management;
- relate marketing theory as contained in this book to everyday marketing situations with which you may come into contact;
- explain how marketers relate to their stakeholders and what the ethical implications of these relationships are;
- discuss aspects of consumer behaviour and explain what is meant by a consumer society;
- explain how marketing affects the natural environment and how 'green marketing' attempts to reduce these effects.

Structure

Book 4 is divided into five study sessions:

Session 1	looks at the nature of marketing, including the meaning of marketing orientation, market segmentation and the concept of relationship marketing.
Session 2	examines the marketing environments that are internal and external to a business, in which the external environment is further divided into the 'micro-environment' and 'macro-environment'.
Session 3	is concerned with customer behaviour and the nature of consumption.
Session 4	introduces the concept of the marketing mix and looks in more detail at products and services, pricing and distribution.
Session 5	covers the responses of business to social and environmental concerns associated with marketing.

Throughout the book, questions of marketing ethics and the impact of marketing on society and the natural environment are also considered.

Session 1 What is marketing?

Why are we studying the question 'what is marketing?'? Most people include advertising, promotions or market research in their definition of marketing. All these are part of marketing practice, but marketing as a general management activity is broader than this. Before you study different aspects of marketing it is important to establish the meaning and scope of marketing.

You will already have had some contact with marketing in some form or another. You may have been involved in marketing something as part of your work, or perhaps as a voluntary activity; for instance, in promoting a charity event. As a consumer you will certainly have had regular contact with the marketing activities of others.

The **aims and objectives** of Session 1 are to:

- explain what is meant by a 'marketing orientation';
- contrast this with other common business orientations;
- explain the purpose of marketing segmentation, targeting and positioning, and what this involves;
- give a brief explanation of marketing information and how this is gathered;
- contrast 'transaction' with 'relationship' marketing.

1.1 The marketing concept

In this first section we will use an activity to reflect on your understanding of marketing. It does not matter if you are new to the subject or have some experience of working in marketing. There is no right answer. It will just help you to identify your current understanding of what marketing is about.

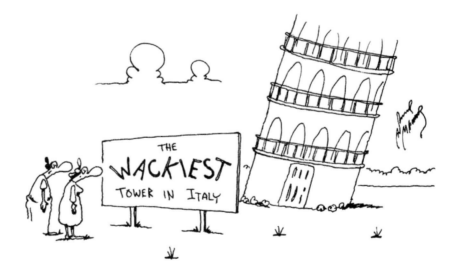

'I liked it better before the marketing people got a hold of it.'

Activity 1.1

Spend about **10–15 minutes** on this activity

Purpose: to draw out your existing understanding of marketing.

Task: before reading any more of this book, write down your answers to the following questions. (Don't feel you need to give 'correct' or 'textbook' answers. The purpose of this activity is to encourage you to formulate your own, preliminary understanding of marketing.)

1   How would you define marketing?

2   What do you think would be the main purpose of the marketing department in a business?

Feedback

1   You may have thought of marketing as a set of particular activities in which marketers engage, such as **market research**, new product development, selling or **advertising**. In a narrow sense this is what is commonly understood by marketing management. Another, broader understanding is that of marketing as a business philosophy; that is, as a general way of doing business which starts with a focus on customer needs and expectations.

2   Marketing management is not solely the domain of the marketing department within a business. Indeed, for marketing to be truly successful it is generally thought that all parts of the business need to have a marketing orientation. The marketing department is responsible for a number of specific marketing activities, but it also often has an important co-ordinating role between other functional areas in order to facilitate a holistic marketing approach.

As we have started to see in Activity 1.1, marketing is more than a particular set of activities carried out by a particular department in a business. In order to be a truly successful marketing organisation, the whole business needs to have a 'marketing orientation'. This means that everybody should have the customers' needs in mind in all their work activities, even if they never have any direct contact with customers. This follows from an understanding that no business would exist without customers and that marketing is a central aspect of the entire business.

Now read the definitions of marketing given below and see how they compare with your answer to Activity 1.1.

Definitions of marketing

There are a number of definitions of marketing, some very concise, some much more detailed. The UK Chartered Institute of Marketing defines marketing in a way which focuses on addressing customer needs:

> Marketing is the management process which identifies, anticipates, and supplies customer requirements efficiently and profitably.

> (Quoted in Blythe, 2001, p. 11)

The following definition, by the American Marketing Association (2004), is complementary but focuses more on the activities of marketers:

> Marketing is an organizational function and a set of processes for creating, communicating, and delivering value to customers and for managing customer relationships in ways that benefit the organization and its stakeholders.

As we shall see later in this section, there are other definitions of marketing, which focus on different aspects, but for the moment it will suffice to think of marketing as a range of activities, carried out by various people in the business, that are designed to understand and satisfy customer needs in a way that allows the business to make a profit or to fulfil other organisational objectives.

A marketing orientation is not the only perspective that a business can adopt. Three other common perspectives (also sometimes called business philosophies or concepts) have been identified: product orientation, production orientation and selling orientation. We look at each of these, and at marketing orientation, in turn below.

Product orientation

Some businesses assume that customers value product quality above all else and that a business that succeeds in producing better products than any of its competitors will have to do little else in order to attract customers and make a profit. Low prices, convenient distribution or convincing selling or advertising become secondary considerations, or even totally unimportant. This 'product orientation' view seems quite convincing for some products. We all know of certain **brands** that have such a high reputation for superior quality and prestige that some people seem quite willing to pay a very high price and travel quite a distance in order to be able to obtain them. Luxury sports cars (such as Lamborghini) or watches (such as Rolex) spring to mind as examples. Normally, however, people do not consider just the quality of a product; they also want value for money and to be able to buy the product in a convenient location. In addition, they may need to be told about the performance of a product and be persuaded, through some form of **promotion,** to buy it.

Production orientation

Businesses operating under the 'production orientation' assume that buyers are very price conscious and are prepared to accept merely adequate quality. These businesses focus on making their production and marketing processes as efficient as possible, so that they can produce large quantities of products at low cost. This usually means mass production of fairly standardised *goods*. This is the business orientation that led Henry Ford to develop the first mass-produced car in the USA in the 1920s, the Ford Model T. There are numerous modern examples of businesses that have succeeded with mass producing standardised goods and selling them cheaply. Fast-food businesses, such as McDonalds, are a good example. However, we can also think of many markets where mass-produced products, even if they are very cheap, are not as successful. Many people, for instance, do not particularly like eating at fast-food restaurants and would prefer to spend a little more for a greater choice of higher quality food. People are often also more concerned with quality than with price when it comes to buying goods that they will use for a long time or on special occasions.

'OK, we've set up the manufacturing facilities, organised the distribution network, hired the marketing expertise, and allocated the advertising budget. Any ideas for a product?'

Selling orientation

Other businesses assume that, no matter how good or cheap a product is, not enough people will buy it unless the business makes a significant selling effort. This is called the 'selling orientation'. Sometimes, businesses operating under this perspective also assume that it is possible to sell almost anything as long as the right sales approach is taken. Selling is often done face-to-face by sales people, but selling via the telephone or the internet increasingly plays a role. This may be appropriate for some products, typically those for which people might have a need but which they would not normally buy unless prompted. Examples include insurance, encyclopaedias or, notoriously, double glazing. On the other hand, the majority of products seem to be sold without such an intensive (and often intrusive) selling effort, and many consumers are becoming annoyed by unsolicited sales approaches. The notion that a good salesperson can sell anything also needs to be treated with some caution. A business that is trying to encourage customers to return to make further purchases in the future will need to be very careful not to oversell its products, thereby provoking irritation or dissatisfaction.

Marketing orientation

The three previous orientations on business and its customers take essentially an 'inside-out' approach, starting with what the business is good at doing (such as high-quality products, efficient production, convincing selling) and what they think customers want. In contrast, the fourth perspective, the 'marketing orientation', takes an 'outside-in' approach, starting with a thorough assessment of the needs and expectations of buyers and then trying to fulfil those needs and expectations in order to attract customers. Although this assessment might lead the business to concentrate on product quality or costs, the crucial difference between this perspective and the product and production orientations is that, from the outset, the business does not merely assume what its potential customers may want, but makes every attempt to find out. In addition, where the selling orientation attempts to change consumers so that they will buy what the business has to sell, the marketing orientation attempts to change the business's offerings in line with what consumers want to buy.

All too often businesses define themselves in terms of the products they make and sell, rather than in terms of what their customers need. In the next activity you will read one of the most influential articles on marketing ever written, 'Marketing myopia' by Theodore Levitt, which will give you a better understanding of what it means to define a business in terms of customer needs.

Activity 1.2

Spend about **90 minutes** on this activity

Purpose: to enhance your understanding of the four business orientations discussed above and relate them to Levitt's article.

Task: read Essential Reading 1, 'Marketing myopia' by Theodore Levitt, which you will find at the back of this book. As you read, make notes and reflect on the following four questions:

1   Which of the four business orientations discussed above did the American railway companies show?

2   How did this orientation manifest itself?

3   According to Levitt, what should they have done differently?

4   Do you think Levitt's recommendation that companies should define themselves in terms of customer needs, rather than in terms of the product they make, is always correct?

Feedback

1   The business philosophy of the American railways, as described by Levitt, can best be characterised as a 'product orientation'.

2   The companies saw themselves as businesses that ran railways, not as businesses that helped people to get from one place to another. This

means they defined themselves in terms of the product they offered, rather than in terms of the need their customers had. For this reason, Levitt argues, they did not foresee the threat of the airline industry.

3   Although he does not call it that, Levitt essentially argues that the railway companies should have adopted a 'marketing orientation'. This means that they should have looked first and foremost at their customers' needs – that is, to get from one place to another as comfortably and quickly as possible – and changed the products they offered accordingly. Levitt seems to suggest that the railway companies could have survived better if they had considered their customers' needs for quick and comfortable transportation and perhaps diversified into air travel.

4   Levitt is certainly correct that businesses must consider their customers' needs in order to do well or even survive. If customers' needs can be better fulfilled by a new, alternative technology, this technology will often overtake an older one. This does not mean that any business can offer any product, though. For instance, running a railway and running an airline are in some respects very different kinds of businesses, and just because a company is good at one does not necessarily mean that it will be good at the other. Technical expertise, as well as understanding markets and customers, is required to be successful.

Activity 1.2 should have increased your understanding of all four of the business 'orientations', but particularly of the marketing orientation.

Before we move on, you will need to familiarise yourself with a few terms that marketers frequently use. These terms are also part of common language but marketers use them in slightly different ways from general language users.

Some marketing terms

You will also find these terms in the Glossary.

Need: a perceived lack of something; an individual not only does not have something but is aware of not having it; a *need* in marketing terms is not the same as a *necessity* – people have far more complex and far reaching needs than mere survival.

Want: a specific satisfier for a need; one may be hungry: that is, in *need* of food, and therefore *want* a roast dinner.

Product: a product is best thought of, not as a specific physical good, such as a car, but as a bundle of benefits, such as the ability to get from A to B, the pleasure of looking at a new, shiny machine, the prestige of owning a desirable make of car, etc.

Customer: a person or business buying a product; also called a *buyer*.

Consumer: a person who actually uses the product or could potentially do so; customers are frequently also consumers and thus the terms may be used interchangeably in some circumstances.

Market: a market consists of all the actual and potential buyers of the business's products. Sometimes the terms market and customers are used interchangeably, but in reality a business's customers are unlikely to be 100% of the market.

(Source: adapted from Kotler et al.,2001)

1.2 Market segmentation, targeting and positioning

A marketing orientation implies that a business must have a good understanding of customer needs and must address the right kinds of customers with the right kinds of products. To make sure that customer needs and product offerings are well matched, marketers normally split up the market into smaller segments, which they can then target with specific product offerings. Grouping customers according to the differences in their needs and behaviour is called *segmentation*. Several assumptions underlie the logic behind segmentation:

- All buyers in a market rarely have exactly the same needs and expectations.
- It is possible to identify smaller subgroups of buyers which are more homogeneous in terms of their needs and expectations.
- It will be easier to satisfy the needs and expectations of these smaller, more homogeneous subgroups of buyers than those of the entire, heterogeneous market.

Once relatively homogeneous market segments have been identified, the business must decide which of these segments it wants to serve. This is called *targeting*. After targeting several segments the business has to position its products so that their perceived qualities and benefits match the needs and expectations of the targeted segment(s).

Market segmentation

Market segmentation is a widespread practice in modern consumer markets. Before the advent of production methods that made cheap mass production of standardised goods possible, consumer goods were typically handmade by artisans, and expensive to buy. Many of these goods, for instance motor cars, were out of the reach of the majority of people, but mass production allowed them to be made cheaply enough so that most people could buy them. Businesses that were able to sell standard products at a low price to large markets were doing well. However, once people had satisfied their initial appetite for these affordable, mass-produced products, they became more discerning. People who already owned a car were less likely to be satisfied with a choice of only one model in one colour (Henry Ford famously quipped that you could buy the Ford Model T in any colour as long as that colour was black).

In the main, businesses could no longer succeed by selling a standard product to everyone: buyers were expecting the product to meet their own requirements more closely. However, offering a customised product or *service* to every single buyer, in the way of handmade products, could not be done with mass-production techniques. Marketers therefore settled on designating potential customers into groups that were small enough to be more homogeneous in their characteristics and expectations, but still large enough to be served profitably with mass-production technologies.

Activity 1.3 below will enable you to apply the idea of market segmentation to your own knowledge of markets.

Activity 1.3

Spend about **10–15 minutes** on this activity

Purpose: to draw out your own knowledge of market segments for some common consumer goods.

Task: try to identify different market segments for one of the following consumer goods:

- shoes and footwear
- toys.

A hint to help you with the answer: market segments for another example, hats, would include men's hats, women's hats, winter hats, summer hats, formal hats, sports hats and similar.

Feedback

Shoes – some common market segments include:

- ladies', men's and children's footwear
- street shoes versus evening shoes
- shoes for various sporting activities
- shoes for different climatic and weather conditions; for example, Wellington boots, snow boots, sandals, and so on.

Toys – some common segments include:

- children's toys versus toys for adults.
- For children we might distinguish between:

     - educational toys

     - cuddly toys

     - dolls

     - construction toys; for example, wooden bricks, Lego, etc.

     - computer and other animated toys

     - toys for different age segments

     - indoor versus outdoor toys.
- For adults, different segments may also be identified; for instance:

     - electric toys, such as electric train sets.

Although it is possible to group people according to many different kinds of criteria, not all such groupings will result in sensible marketing segments.

In order to be viable, market segments need to be:

Measurable It must be possible to define who the members of the segment are and how many of them there are.

Accessible Marketers must have some way of communicating with the chosen segment.

Substantial The segments must be large enough to be worth aiming for.

Congruent The members of the segments must have fairly similar requirements with respect to this type of product.

Stable The nature and membership of the segment must be reasonably constant.

(Source: adapted from Blythe, 2001)

It is generally impractical for marketers to ask every potential customer about their preferences. Marketers therefore tend to group people into segments according to general criteria which are thought or known to influence their preferences for particular products. Four types of criteria commonly used for segmentation are 'geographic', 'demographic', 'psychographic' and 'behavioural' segmentation (Kotler et al., 2001). These are defined below.

Geographic segmentation

This type of segmentation groups potential customers according to where they live because different geographical locations vary with regard to climate, for example. Geographic segmentation therefore makes sense when a product, such as cold weather clothing, is suited only to certain types of locations; when the product does not travel well, such as highly perishable fruit or fragile sheet glass; or when a business has only limited funds and therefore decides to focus on one location to start with.

Demographic segmentation

This type of segmentation groups people according to factors such as age, gender, lifestyle, education and economy. This is because people's needs often vary with their demographic characteristics. Demographic segmentation, apart from its usefulness in predicting many types of buying behaviour, is popular with marketers because it is relatively easy to do. Governments and both official and semi-official agencies often collect extensive data on the demographic composition of populations, as well as their lifestyles and consumer preferences, and this data is easily accessible to businesses.

Psychographic segmentation

This type of segmentation groups potential customers according to their beliefs, attitudes and opinions, as well as their psychological characteristics. A *financial services* business might offer different investment products depending on whether people are risk takers or risk averse. Psychology is often quite a good predictor of people's consumer preferences, but, unlike attitudes and opinions, psychological traits are difficult to measure for large populations.

Behavioural segmentation

This type of segmentation groups people according to the way in which they use, and benefit from, the product. Car drivers might be segmented into business and private users. Private car users might be further segmented depending on the main purpose for which they use their car, such as commuting, domestic purposes or leisure activities. Different types of vehicles may be appropriate for these different uses. Behavioural segments are often more easily accessible, as there may be specialist media dedicated to them, such as outdoor magazines or magazines addressing parents with children.

Targeting segments

Once they have segmented the market, businesses must decide how many and which segments they want to sell to. They may target the most profitable segments, or segments that are currently not well served, or a segment whose needs match the specific capabilities of the business most closely.

At a generic level, there are three principal targeting strategies that marketers can pursue:

1 *Niche marketing* The business concentrates on a single segment. This makes sense if a business is quite small and does not have the resources to target several segments, or if the business has unique know-how or other capabilities that allow it to serve the needs of this segment particularly well.

2 *Differentiated marketing* The business concentrates on two or more segments, with differentiated product offerings for each segment. For

instance, most large car manufacturers target several segments with different types and sizes of cars.

3   *Undifferentiated marketing (also called mass marketing)* Selling one basic product to the entire market is still a common and successful strategy in some product categories. The market for petrol remains largely undifferentiated, for example.

In summary, small businesses with limited resources can often succeed only by concentrating on a single or very few segments. Large businesses with many resources, on the other hand, may be able to pursue a differentiated strategy successfully, but may be reluctant to service very small segments with limited profit potential. These segments can then often be targeted successfully by smaller businesses.

Positioning the business's offerings

Once the owners of the business have decided which market segments they want to target, they need to make sure that product offerings are perceived to meet the needs and expectations of those segments. In other words, there is a need to 'position' products or services in line with these needs and expectations. What counts here is how customers define important product attributes and perceive the business and what it has to offer. Marketers can influence this positioning by manipulating the ***marketing mix***. The marketing mix is discussed in greater detail in study Session 4 of this book.

We have suggested that most businesses today segment their markets and then target one or several of these segments by positioning their products or services so as to meet the needs of the target segment(s). Not all businesses, however, do this. For some small businesses, such as a bespoke tailor, who know their customers personally, it may still be possible to design the product or service specifically to each individual customer's wishes. Modern information technology (IT) has also made a certain degree of 'mass tailoring' possible. For instance, a car manufacturer might adapt several basic car designs individually according to the specific wishes of each customer, by using computer technology to programme these specifications directly into the production machinery. This will be more expensive than producing cars to a standard template for larger segments, but much cheaper than making a car individually, by hand, for each customer.

Ethical issues in market segmentation

Certain segmentation and targeting practices can result in ethical problems, particularly where vulnerable consumers are targeted. These include children, who are less able to evaluate marketing claims, some older consumers who find it difficult to deal with the fast pace of modern economic life, as well as economically deprived consumers, who suffer disproportionally if they are sold products with misleading claims or excessive prices. It is thought that producers have a particular duty of care towards these vulnerable consumers, who may be less able to defend their own rights and interests. Sometimes marketers have been accused of deliberately targeting low-quality or harmful products, such as high-strength alcoholic drinks, at these vulnerable groups

(Smith and Cooper-Martin, 1997). The opposite problem arises when certain services are withheld from particular target markets. For instance, banks have been accused of automatically denying credit to any consumer from low-income areas, because of the perceived higher risk of non-repayment, without taking the specific circumstances of individual consumers into account (Crane and Matten, 2004).

1.3 Marketing information

You will already have realised that, in order to be successful, businesses need to be well informed, not only about the needs and expectations of their current and potential customers, but also about other market actors and wider economic and social forces. There are many ways of gaining marketing information; formal market research is just one of them. These different ways of gathering and analysing information are sometimes called a business's *marketing information system*. Some businesses have highly formalised marketing information systems whereas others gather and analyse information in a more informal way. This depends partly on the size of the business and on the competitiveness of the market.

Most businesses find it difficult to gather all the information they need, differentiate important from less important information and analyse incoming information in the most effective and efficient way. Many find that they have simultaneously too much and not enough information. This means that, although they gather a lot of information on a regular basis, some collected specifically and some unsolicited, it is often not easy to distinguish the most important detail. As a result, whenever marketing decisions are to be made, managers will probably find that they have or can obtain some but not all the necessary or desirable information. Even in a business with a very good marketing information system many decisions will have to be based on incomplete information.

There are three main sources of marketing information:

1 *Internal records* These comprise relevant marketing information gathered from sources within the business, such as sales records, complaints records, information from loyalty schemes, etc.

2 *Marketing intelligence* This is everyday information about developments in the marketing environment, gathered through publicly available sources of information, informal talks, observations, etc.

3 *Marketing research* This is formal research aimed at gathering specific data to help solve a particular marketing problem. It includes both secondary and primary market research (which we discuss further below).

Internal information is often quick and easy to obtain as it is already available within the business. However, as this information is normally gathered for different purposes it may be only partially suitable for the current situation.

Marketing intelligence comes from many different sources, the most important of which is often the knowledge and observations of people working in the business. Senior managers of the business may be members of the same clubs as the executives of the business's suppliers, customers or competitors. Sales people come into regular contact with current and potential customers and can gain valuable information, not only about these customers, but also about competitors who may be dealing with the same customers. New staff who may have worked for competitors, customers or suppliers are also a very valuable source of marketing intelligence. Much of this is not very systematic but it may be extensive. It is therefore worthwhile for a business to develop a systematic way of using this knowledge.

The most formal and specific way of gathering marketing information is market research. The business can use already existing information which perhaps it has bought from external sources, such as external market reports, but which sometimes is also freely available, such as government statistics. This is called secondary data collection. Primary data collection, on the other hand, gathers data directly from potential customers, usually with a specific marketing problem in mind. This is the form of marketing information that is most suitable for obtaining very specific information for a particular problem, but it is typically complex and expensive. It is usually used only if other sources of information prove insufficient and if the information need is sufficiently great.

1.4 Transaction and relationship marketing

In this last section of this study session we look briefly at the idea of 'relationship marketing'. This has become an important part of our understanding of marketing.

Market segmentation and targeting and the use of the marketing mix to position the brand and attract customers have become the mainstream of marketing theory (Grönroos, 1990). Essentially, this approach focuses on the final point of attracting customers and achieving a transaction (that is, an exchange of the business's product against the customer's money). Repeat business is, of course, not ruled out and is even desired but, implicitly at least, the main emphasis is on this first transaction. Since the 1990s this 'transaction marketing' approach has been increasingly criticised on the basis that it pays little attention to ongoing, long-term relationships between buyers and sellers. Yet, for many types of marketing it is as important, if not more so, to cultivate these relationships as it is to get the marketing mix right. Businesses that sell to other businesses and businesses that provide services have engaged in 'relationship marketing' for some time.

In contrast to the definitions of marketing given in section 1.1 in study Session 1 above, Grönroos defines marketing in the following way: 'Marketing is to establish, maintain and enhance … relationships with customers and other partners, at a profit, so that objectives of the parties involved are met' (Grönroos, 1990, p. 138).

Factors driving relationship marketing

Francis Buttle (1996) argues that the increased attention to relationship marketing since the 1990s has been driven by a number of factors:

- More intense, often global competition has meant that businesses have needed methods of differentiating themselves from their competitors in ways that go beyond the traditional marketing mix.

- Many markets have become fragmented into smaller and smaller segments and thus traditional market segmentation has reached its limits.

- Product quality has become generally high and businesses have found it increasingly difficult to compete on superior quality alone as most competitors are able to offer similar quality. This is forcing businesses to seek *competitive advantage* in other ways.

- Customers have become more demanding and are not as *brand loyal*. That is, they are willing to change suppliers frequently in order to get the best deal. To keep their customers, businesses therefore need to pay extra attention to them.

Close, personal relationships between buyers and sellers were a feature of most traditional markets before the introduction of mass production and mass-marketing techniques. Today, relationship marketing is particularly relevant in those instances where buyers and sellers are able to get to know each other; for example, in services marketing and in business-to-business marketing. Attempts have also been made to introduce relationship marketing into other consumer markets: one form of relationship marketing to consumers with which you may be familiar is the 'loyalty card' issued by many large retailers. It is unclear, however, whether most consumers actually want a 'relationship' with, say, their supermarket.

There are good economic reasons why marketers should pay attention to their relationships with customers. First, it is more expensive to win new customers than it is to retain old ones and, second, a relationship with a customer tends to become more profitable for a business the longer it continues. A key aspect of relationship marketing is therefore to try to avoid customer defections.

Activity 1.4

Spend about **20 minutes** on this activity

Purpose: to relate the concept of relationship marketing to your own experience of marketing practice.

Task: think of the dealings that you, as a consumer, have with different businesses. In other words, think of businesses with which you could say you have a 'marketing relationship' and try to answer the following questions:

1   Which of these are ongoing or long-term?

2   Have any of these businesses made any special efforts to maintain their marketing relationship with you?

3   Why do you keep going back to them?

Feedback

Your answer will depend on your particular experiences.

1 Businesses with which you might have a longer term marketing relationship could include service providers, such as banks, lawyers, hairdressers and car service businesses; or retailers, such as small family-run grocery stores, specialty stores (for example, for sports equipment) or even supermarkets.

2/3 Increasingly, businesses make special efforts to retain their customers and keep marketing relationships going. They may send out newsletters to their regular customers and provide discount vouchers based on previous purchases. Not all businesses do this formally, however, and the relationship with many smaller businesses may well be based on informal chats and good advice and service.

According to Buttle (1996), healthy marketing relationships are characterised by concern, trust, commitment and service. Concern means that marketers should be concerned for the welfare of their customers and other stakeholders, meeting or even exceeding their expectations and producing customer satisfaction or even delight.

Trust means that one partner has confidence in the other's reliability, and commitment means that a business wants to maintain a relationship. Trust and commitment have to be earned by a business through its concern for its partner's welfare and its dedication to delivering a good service. In return, the business hopes for a certain degree of loyalty from the partner.

1.5 Conclusion

In this study session you have learnt that marketing is more than just a set of techniques, certainly much more than advertising or selling. At its most fundamental, marketing is best seen as a particular orientation of business, which takes customer needs and expectations as its starting point and designs the business's product or service offerings so that they meet these needs and expectations.

You have also learnt how businesses segment markets and use marketing information to understand and target their actual and potential customers. In order to be better able to meet their customers' needs and expectations, marketers tend to split a larger market into smaller, more homogeneous segments. They can then target one or more of these segments by positioning their product offerings so that they meet the segment's needs and expectations fairly closely. Marketing intelligence, which includes but is not limited to market research, is used by businesses to gain the information that they need to assess customer needs and expectations.

Finally, you have learnt that marketing is not just focused on achieving individual transactions with buyers, but is increasingly seen as a series of ongoing relationships. Relationship marketing implies businesses' concern for the welfare of their customers, mutual trust and commitment to the relationship, and a desire on the part of businesses to provide excellent service.

In the next study session you will learn how the marketing environment influences the needs and expectations of the customers of a business and the business's ability to meet these.

1.6 Learning outcomes

By the end of this study session on the nature of marketing you should be able to:

- differentiate between and compare a marketing orientation and product, production and selling orientations;
- discuss the meaning of market segmentation, the reasons why businesses segment their markets and the main bases for segmentation, as well as the main targeting strategies used by businesses;
- describe the nature of a marketing intelligence system and the different ways in which a business can gather marketing intelligence;
- differentiate between transaction and relationship marketing and appreciate some of the rationales behind relationship marketing.

You will have developed your learning by:

- completing and reflecting on the activities in this study session;
- reading the seminal marketing article by Theodore Levitt (Essential Reading 1) and carrying out the activity associated with it.

Session 2 Understanding marketing environments

Why are we studying 'understanding marketing environments'?
Businesses must have a thorough understanding of their customers in order to be successful. However, they need to understand more than just their customers. They also need to have a good understanding of the marketing environment at large as this has a significant influence, not only on customers' needs and expectations, but also on the business's ability to satisfy these.

The **aims and objectives** of Session 2 are to:

- explain what is meant by the marketing environment;

- explain the difference between the macro- and the micro-environment, their elements, and how they affect marketing practice;

- explain the ethical issues related to businesses' relationships with key market stakeholders.

2.1 The internal and micro-environments

The marketing environment is the business environment from a marketing point of view. Marketers tend to divide the marketing environment into internal and external environments, where the external environment is further divided into the 'micro-environment' and the 'macro-environment'.
Figure 2.1 shows the different elements of the marketing environment.

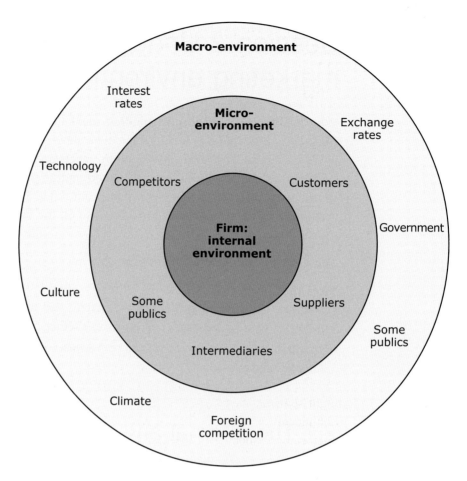

Figure 2.1 The marketing environment (Source: Blythe, 2001, p. 18, Figure 2.1)

Ethical issues apply to all aspects of business. Marketing has, however, more relationships with external stakeholders than most other business functions and ethical issues become much more visible. You will learn about ethical issues in a business's relationship with key market stakeholders throughout study Sessions 2 and 3.

The internal environment

In the previous study session you learnt that marketing affects the entire business. The marketing department has to work closely with other functional departments in the business, such as research and development (R&D), purchasing, production or finance, to ensure that customer needs and expectations are considered at all stages of the business process. For example, a production manager and their staff will normally concentrate on the specific tasks of production such as meeting production targets, maintaining an even workload for the machinery, and so on. As they often do not have regular contact with customers it is easy for them to forget about customer concerns. Marketers have to persuade employees throughout the business that customer orientation is a key consideration.

The micro-environment

The micro-environment consists of individuals and organisations that are in direct contact with the business. They include existing and potential customers, suppliers, competitors, intermediaries and some other stakeholders. Of these, customers are the most important from a marketing point of view. They are, therefore, considered separately in study Session 3.

Competitors

Businesses need to understand their competitors. Meeting customer needs and expectations is not enough if competitors can do it better. To understand competitors a business needs to define who its competitors actually are. As you saw in Essential Reading 1 by Levitt, which you studied for Activity 1.2, businesses often define their competition too narrowly and only consider those other businesses which offer the same or a very similar product.

How, then, should a business define its competition? Taking the widest definition, all businesses compete with all other businesses for a share of customers' money. If people decide to buy a new car in one year they may then not want to or be able to afford an expensive holiday in the same year. More immediate competitors depend on the market segment that the business is targeting. As segments have different needs and expectations the business may face different sources of competition in different segments. A bookseller might segment their customers into those seeking entertainment and those seeking information. In the first case, competition would include that from other entertainment industries, such as cinema, whereas in the second case other sources of information, such as the internet, would need to be considered.

One useful way of analysing the type and severity of competition in an industry has been suggested by Michael Porter (1990) in his 'five forces model' of competition. In this model not only current providers of the same product are seen as competitive forces, but also potential new providers of the same product, as well as providers of existing and potential substitute products. Substitutes are different products that give a similar benefit. Air and rail travel are substitutes for medium-length journeys. The greater the threat from either of these forces the more intense the competitive pressure. Likewise, if suppliers and buyers are in a strong bargaining position, perhaps because they are very large in size or have a near *monopoly* position, this is likely to put more competitive pressure on the businesses in the industry. Porter's 'five forces model' is explained in more detail in Essential Reading 2 which is the focus of the next activity.

Activity 2.1

Spend about **90 minutes** on this activity

Purpose: to consolidate your understanding of the competitive forces faced by any business.

Task: read Essential Reading 2, 'How competitive forces shape strategy' by Michael E. Porter, which you will find at the back of this book. This should take about 60 of the 90 minutes suggested for this activity. As you read, make notes for your own learning and revision purposes and use your learning from the article to tackle the following business scenario. Imagine you are about to open a new café near where you live. How tough is your competition likely to be? Try to answer the following questions:

1 Who would be your existing competitors?

2 How high is the threat of new entrants?

3 What are the likely substitute services and products?

4 How strong is the bargaining power of suppliers likely to be?

5 How strong is the bargaining power of customers likely to be?

Feedback

1 Existing competitors would be other restaurants and cafés, as well as pubs offering food. These could be located either in the town itself or in surrounding villages, or in other towns that are within easy driving distance.

2 As a new business you are, of course, a new entrant yourself. The six major barriers to entry that Porter mentions are not likely to be very high for a small café. This is good news for you but it also means that other new entrants are likely. This means that there could be quite a lot of direct competition for your business.

3 Substitutes could be fast-food outlets, home delivery services and ready meals that can be bought from supermarkets.

4 As a small business you may find that large suppliers (for food ingredients, kitchen utensils, plates, cutlery, etc.) have quite a bit of bargaining power over you. You may be in a stronger position to bargain with smaller, local suppliers or perhaps by buying ingredients directly from farmers.

5 The bargaining power of customers will depend on the number and attractiveness of existing competitors, as well as the availability and attractiveness of substitutes. If there are a lot of existing restaurants and cafés already in the area, you will have to work harder to attract and please customers. If there is a good supply of home delivery or quick-to-prepare meals from local supermarkets, people may be more tempted to use these as substitutes for restaurant meals.

Ethical issues in competitor relations

One might ask why a business should recognise any specific ethical claims by its competitors if these are competing for the same rewards in the marketplace. However, competitors are affected by what a business does and, in turn, have a significant ability to affect that business. Competitors are given legal rights in many countries and also have certain moral rights; for instance, the right to privacy or the right to 'fair play' (Crane and Matten, 2004).

Showing a level of ethical behaviour towards competitors does not mean that businesses should not compete actively and vigorously with each other. On the contrary, attempts to reduce competition in a market are often *un*ethical as they can be disadvantageous to customers. Ethical problems in a business's dealings with its competitors arise either because of overly aggressive competition or, conversely, because of insufficient competition. Overly aggressive competition can be seen in underhand ways of collecting information about competitors, in 'dirty tricks' and in the deliberate attempt to put competitors out of business.

'Dirty tricks' include negative advertising, where a business deliberately attempts to damage the reputation of a competitor's products or business practices. 'Stealing customers' using underhand methods, such as bribery, misleading claims or similar, is another questionable tactic. So is 'predatory pricing', where a business sets its prices below its own cost with the sole or main intention of driving competitors out of the market. Some of these behaviours seem quite extreme but none is unheard of in contemporary business practice. British Airways' 'dirty war' against Virgin Atlantic in the 1990s involved accessing confidential passenger information, poaching customers as they queued for Virgin tickets, stealing documents, a smear campaign in the press and other aggressive measures (Crane and Matten, 2004).

Suppliers

Suppliers are 'businesses and individuals that provide the resources needed by the business and its competitors to produce goods and services' (Kotler et al., 2001, p. 119). They are an important link in the overall system that delivers value to customers.

Many larger businesses have specialist purchasing departments which deal with suppliers on a day-to-day basis. It is important for any business to monitor supply quality and availability. In the short run, supply shortages can cost sales in that the business cannot deliver, and low-quality supplies can lead to low-quality final products and complaints from customers. In the long run, supply problems can damage customer satisfaction and lead to customers moving to competitors.

There are different ways of managing suppliers. Some businesses take the approach of always trying to buy the cheapest supplies possible, driving hard bargains and frequently switching suppliers. Many businesses use this approach for less critical supplies, such as stationery and cleaning materials. For more important resources, however, many businesses prefer a relationship approach. By building long-term relationships with a smaller number of suppliers they can ensure reliability of supply, both in terms of quality and delivery. Sometimes businesses also have to co-operate with suppliers to develop the kind of resources they need; for instance, to develop specialist machinery which is not currently available in the market. This kind of co-operation usually leads to long-term supply relationships as both the buying and the selling business have invested much in the technology and the relationship and cannot easily afford to switch.

Ethical issues in supplier relationships

Ethical issues in business–supplier relationships generally stem from unequal power between the two partners. Large supermarkets, for instance, often have greater power than both producers of goods, particularly small farmers, and consumers. You may already have heard the claim that, due to their buying power, UK supermarket chains can exploit farmers by paying very low prices for meat and vegetables, but not passing on these low prices to their customers. Crane and Matten (2004) point out that abuses of power over suppliers often have negative consequences for the purchasing business itself as they may jeopardise quality and reliability of supplies in the long run. However, short-term profit advantages may tempt a business to abuse its power over suppliers.

Ethical issues in supplier relations also relate to the negotiations between a business and its potential suppliers. While both sides will try to get as good a deal as possible, there are negotiating tactics, such as deception, which are considered unethical or at least questionable by many people. Reitz et al. (1998) suggest that engaging in these tactics can lead to damaged buyer–supplier relationships, thus also jeopardising long-term security of supply. By negotiating in unethical ways, businesses may sully their reputation and lose future opportunities, as suppliers will not be willing to discuss new ideas.

Marketing intermediaries

Marketing intermediaries are businesses that help another business to promote, sell and distribute its goods to final buyers. They include:

- *resellers*: individuals and businesses that buy goods and services to resell;
- *physical distribution businesses*: warehouse, transportation and other businesses that help a business to stock and move goods from their points of origin to their destination;
- *marketing services agencies*: marketing research businesses, advertising agencies, media businesses, marketing consulting businesses and other service providers that help a business to target and promote its products to the right markets;

• *financial intermediaries*: banks, credit businesses, insurance businesses and other businesses that help finance transactions or insure against the risks associated with the buying and selling of goods.

(Adapted from Kotler et al., 2001, p. 120)

Like suppliers, marketing intermediaries are an important part of the system that delivers value to customers.

Activity 2.2

Spend about **15 minutes** on this activity

Purpose: to encourage you to think about the use of marketing intermediaries.

Task: imagine you are working for a publishing house that specialises in publishing academic textbooks. What kind of marketing intermediaries could you use to help you reach your customers?

Feedback

You will probably have found that you could use a mixture of ways to reach your customers, including:

• *No intermediaries (or resellers)* Publishers can and do sell directly to customers, via their paper or web-based catalogues, taking orders in writing, over the telephone or through their web pages.

• *Traditional bookshops* Most academic texts continue to be sold in this way.

• *Internet retailers* More and more books are sold by internet retailers, such as Amazon.

• *Universities* Sometimes lecturers buy textbooks in bulk and sell them on to their students, passing on the discount they receive.

No matter which resellers a publisher uses, they will need the services of a physical distribution company to get the books to customers or resellers. They may also use the services of marketing research or advertising agencies and may need financial services, such as business loans or insurance.

Other stakeholders

Stakeholders are individuals, groups of individuals and organisations that have an actual or potential interest in the business because they are affected by and/or have the ability to affect the business's pursuit of its own objectives (Freeman, 1984). In marketing textbooks stakeholders are often called '***publics***' but we will use the more widely used and understood term 'stakeholders'. Businesses have many stakeholders who are interested in their marketing activities. A business that is marketing sweet drinks to children may, for instance, attract criticism from child nutritionists or children's charities.

Often businesses look at these stakeholders strategically. That means that they identify any support that they may need from a stakeholder or any potential threat that the stakeholder may pose, and then try to manage stakeholder relationships in such a way that they can maximise the support and minimise the threat.

2.2 The macro-environment

The macro-environment consists of the 'larger society forces that affect the whole micro-environment' (Kotler et al., 2001, p. 118), including demographic, economic, natural, social, political, legal, cultural and technological forces. The widely accepted STEEP (sociological, technological, economic, environmental, political) model offers one way of classifying these factors. They often have a strong influence on marketing, either because they impact on buyer behaviour or because they impact directly on the ability of businesses to respond to this buyer behaviour.

Sociological factors

There are many aspects which fall under sociological factors in marketing and which are of potential importance to marketers. Some of them are listed below.

Demographic factors

- population size
- growth trends
- age structure
- education levels
- family structures.

Social factors

- impact of social class
- impact of family and other social groupings
- roles of men and women
- attitudes toward divorce and single parenthood.

Cultural factors

- language
- ethnicity
- religion
- national culture
- globalisation
- increased migration
- continued cultural differences between and within nations.

Demography is the study of human populations; it looks at, for example, population size and growth trends, the age structure of a population, family structures, education levels and population diversity. In Western societies some notable changes have taken place in all these areas over recent decades. After initial strong population growth in the 1960s, after the ravages of the Second World War, birth rates in many countries started to fall. At the same time improvements in living standards, hygiene and medical care meant that people now live longer. Therefore, many Western populations are shrinking in overall size and at the same time are ageing. Family structures have also changed significantly.

In the 1950s the nuclear family, with mother, father and two or three children, where the father worked full time and the mother stayed at home to look after the children, was considered the norm (although the reality may always have been a bit more diverse). This has changed as social norms have changed. For example, divorce and childbirth outside traditional marriages have become far less socially stigmatised, and more people live alone and in single parent households.

Activity 2.3

Spend about **30 minutes** on this activity

Purpose: to think about demographic trends and factors that are familiar to you and how they may affect marketing practice.

Task: think about some common products that you and your family buy (such as groceries, clothing, household items, newspapers and magazines). Now think about ways in which the marketing of these products could be affected by the following demographic trends:

1   lower birth rates

2   ageing population

3   increased education levels

4   smaller household sizes.

Feedback

1 *Lower birth rates* Producers of baby products have a smaller overall market size in terms of population (this may be counterbalanced however, by parents spending more money on each child).

2 *Ageing population* Marketers who target older age segments, such as providers of specialist holidays for people over fifty, have a larger overall market size.

3 *Increased education levels* In many industrialised and industrialising societies, more people are educated to a higher level. More women have careers before having children and people get married later, which has indirect effects on marketing in terms of fewer births and smaller household sizes. More direct marketing implications include a greater market for educational goods and changing tastes in a wide variety of products ranging from food to entertainment and holiday destinations.

4 *Smaller household sizes* As people get married later, bring up children in single parent households and live longer there are more single and smaller households. This has meant increased demand for smaller packs of household and food items and for the provision of more day-long childcare facilities or after school clubs, to name just two examples.

Sociological and demographic trends are often interconnected. Many of the demographic shifts described above are the result of sociological changes, such as those suggested above. Other social aspects of interest to marketers include social class, which often has a profound impact on people's tastes and consumption habits. Similarly, people are generally quite strongly influenced by the views of their immediate social group, such as family and friends.

Cultural differences are of greatest importance to international marketers, but even within one national market there are often significant cultural differences. Examples include people of different ethnic origin (referring not only to those of immigrant origin, but also to existing cultural groupings within a nation state, such as the English, Scottish, Welsh and Northern Irish within the UK, or cultural differences between, for example, northern and southern England) and different age groups: you may have noticed that your values and opinions, for instance, may be quite different from those held by your parents' generation. Cultural differences may also exist between different religions, or between men and women. Some products are more sensitive to cultural differences than others. Food and clothing, for example, are often considered to be particularly culturally sensitive, because even after immigrating to another country, people often continue eat the kind of food they would have eaten, and to wear the kind of clothing they would have worn, in their home country. However, **cultural sensitivity** can also be found in less obvious products, such as financial services.

Technological factors

Technology influences businesses' capacity to offer products, as well as consumers' ability to use them. 'Technology' refers to all the ways in which humans work upon and modify their environment, and it changes all the time. One of the most visible technological shifts of recent decades has been the widespread application and availability of information technology. Personal computers and mobile phones have become common consumer items and have opened up a huge market, not just for these products themselves but for all sorts of associated hardware and software. Computerised technology has changed nearly all other large consumer products as well, ranging from microwave ovens, to televisions and cars.

Technological and social factors are often closely interwoven. For instance, increased worldwide migration and the increased ethnic diversity in many countries, as well as overall globalisation trends, have only been made possible by a huge increase in worldwide communication and transport. The development of reliable methods of birth control has greatly contributed to changing birth rates and population age structures.

Economic factors

From a marketer's perspective the most important aspect of the economic environment is its capacity to influence consumer buying power and spending patterns. When a country experiences an economic depression and consumer purchasing power is reduced, people spend their money more carefully. They usually seek greater value in the products and services they buy and are less willing to pay for 'frills' they consider non-essential. Under unfavourable economic circumstances a greater proportion of people's incomes is spent on 'necessities', such as food, housing and transport, and a smaller proportion is spent on 'luxuries', such as holidays or meals out.

The economic policies pursued by governments and other economic policy makers often have quite direct impacts on people's *available income* and thus purchasing power. Due to the high rate of home ownership, interest rates in the UK have a big impact on most people's available income. An increase in the general rate of interest means that people have to pay higher monthly interest on their mortgages from the same level of income, and they therefore have less income available to spend on other things.

Natural environmental forces

For many years business operated as if natural resources were unlimited and any impact of business activity could be absorbed easily and indefinitely by the natural environment. Increasingly, we know that this is not the case and natural environmental forces are becoming an important consideration for businesses. On the one hand, marketing and consumption activities have a significant impact on the natural environment. On the other hand, changes in the natural environment can equally significantly affect businesses' capacity to meet customer requirements. Marketing is influenced by and has an impact on the natural environment at every stage in the production and consumption process, from the sourcing of raw materials, through the production of goods and services and storing and transportation of finished goods, to the use of the product by the final consumer and its eventual disposal.

The Earth's natural resources provide us with the air we breathe, the water we drink and use for many other purposes, the plants and animals we eat, the materials from which we build our houses, make our clothes and construct our tools, and the energy we need for heating, transportation and industrial production. If these resources are being used or made unusable at a faster rate than natural processes can replenish them, human quality of life must deteriorate in the long run. If they are distributed unequally between people, as they generally are, quality of life deteriorates faster for some people than for others, but ultimately it deteriorates for everybody (Diamond, 2005). Figure 2.2 gives a graphical representation of how businesses use environmental resources and release wastes into the environment at different stages of the business process.

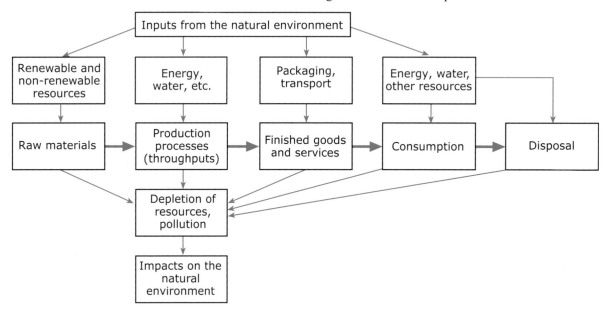

Figure 2.2 Business and the natural environment

Political factors

Political factors refer to laws, government agencies and pressure groups as they influence and constrain the actions of business and consumers. All markets are to some extent regulated by government action; otherwise monopolies tend to develop, which greatly reduce the ability of producers and consumers to participate freely in those markets. Some countries try to regulate only the barest minimum; for instance, to rule against monopolies and cartels (that is, illegal agreements between competing businesses to limit competition: for example, through price fixing). Others actively intervene in the running of industry. In capitalist economies laws that regulate business behaviour are passed for three main reasons: to protect businesses from each other – for example, to prevent cartels and monopolies and to limit unfair competition; to protect consumers from unfair practices, such as deceptive advertising or unsafe products; and to protect the interests of society as a whole from the negative consequences of unrestrained business behaviour.

Businesses need to be aware of legislation relating to their products and services. There are laws and regulations relating to production processes, as well as to the ways in which goods and services may be marketed. For instance, in the European Union pharmaceutical businesses may not advertise prescription drugs directly to patients, and tobacco and alcohol may not be advertised to children. There are also many restrictions on the use of finished goods by consumers; for example, gardeners may use garden pesticides only in approved ways.

Public interest groups are an increasingly important political factor. Many pressure groups exist for the sole or main purpose of monitoring and exerting pressure on businesses. Consumer rights groups watch for unfair treatment of consumers by businesses, and environmental groups exert pressure on businesses to reduce their impact on the natural environment. Pressure groups may deal directly with businesses, but they often also operate through lobbying government or addressing themselves to consumers.

2.3 Conclusion

In this study session you have looked at the business environment from a marketing point of view. You have learnt the distinction between the internal, the micro- and the macro-environment and how each influences a business's marketing activities. You have also learnt about key elements in the micro-environment (customers, suppliers, competitors, intermediaries, other stakeholders) and the macro-environment (STEEP factors). Understanding how these environmental factors influence customer expectations as well as a business's ability to meet these expectations is crucial for business success. In this study session we have not yet looked at customers and their behaviour. We will turn to this in the next study session.

2.4 Learning outcomes

By the end of this study session on marketing environments you should be able to:

- differentiate between internal, micro- and macro-environments;
- discuss business's relationships with competitors, suppliers, intermediaries and other stakeholders, as well as the ethical issues associated with those relationships;
- discuss the elements of the STEEP model in terms of how it relates to a business's marketing activities.

You will have developed your learning by:

- reading and making notes on the article by Michael Porter (Essential Reading 2), and discussing its implications for a practical marketing situation.

Session 3 Understanding customers and consumption

Why are we studying 'understanding customers and consumption'?
Customers are the most important constituents of marketers. Without customers there would be no business. This also applies to not-for-profit and public sector organisations that cannot survive for long if they are not seen to serve their primary service users well. Businesses therefore need a thorough understanding of customers and their behaviour, as well as an understanding of how consumption fits into contemporary social life.

The **aims and objectives** of Session 3 are to:

- outline the different types of buyer behaviour;
- explain the complex buying decision process;
- discuss the differences between consumer and business buying behaviour;
- compare the rational approach to understanding customers and a social and cultural understanding of consumption;
- describe three main aspects of cultural and social functions of consumption.

3.1 The rational approach to understanding customers

It is usual in the marketing literature to distinguish between consumer marketing and business-to-business marketing. In this section we will look at both these types of customers in turn.

Consumer buying behaviour

There are a number of different academic approaches to understanding consumer behaviour. According to Belk (1995), a 'rational' approach has been most influential in marketing. This assumes that consumers tend to make rational choices about the products and services they buy and use. This approach is concerned with understanding how individual consumers evaluate and choose products, so that marketers can tailor their offerings more effectively to consumer needs and expectations. More recently, another approach to understanding consumer behaviour has arisen, which is more concerned with consumption as a wider social and cultural phenomenon, rather than with the decision-making processes of individual consumers. This approach will be discussed later in this study session.

Figure 3.1 represents a simple model of consumer behaviour, depicting influences on consumer buying behaviour, buyer decision processes and buyer responses. The model does not go into detail on what goes on inside the buyer's mind – it treats this as a 'black box'; that is, something which is known to exist but the internal workings of which are unknown. In fact, quite a lot is known about what goes on in this black box and other, more complex models of consumer behaviour capture some of this. The model shown in Figure 3.1 assumes that there are two main types of external influence on consumers: market stimuli (the marketing offerings of different businesses) and elements of the business environment, as depicted in the STEEP model outlined in the previous study session.

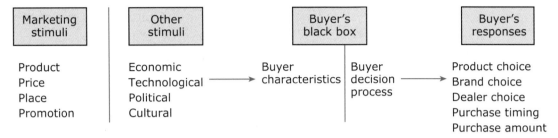

Figure 3.1 Model of consumer behaviour (Source: Kotler et al., 2001, p. 191, Figure 6.1)

Types of consumer buying behaviour

Consumers do not all make buying decisions in the same way. Depending on the type of product being bought, they search for more or less information on the product beforehand and spend varying amounts of time assessing this information. Assael (1987) distinguishes between four types of consumer buying behaviour:

1 complex buying behaviour

2 dissonance-reducing buying behaviour

3 habitual buying behaviour

4 variety-seeking buying behaviour.

Which kind of behaviour consumers engage in depends on how involved they are in a particular purchase. This partly depends on their personality and partly on the kind of purchase being made. The type of buyer behaviour also depends on whether or not consumers can see significant differences between the brands on offer. For instance, there may be quite considerable differences between the durability of different washing machines, but this is difficult for consumers to tell in advance. Figure 3.2 shows Assael's four types of buying behaviour.

	High involvement	Low involvement
Significant differences between brands	Complex buying behaviour	Variety-seeking buying behaviour
Few differences between brands	Dissonance-reducing buying behaviour	Habitual buying behaviour

Figure 3.2 Types of buying behaviour (Source: Kotler et al., 2001, p. 212, Figure 6.5)

According to Assael (1987), 'complex buying behaviour' is characterised by high consumer involvement and significant differences between brands. It tends to occur when a purchase is expensive, risky or purchased infrequently, or when consumers use the product to express themselves. A house is a very good example; cars, computers, or a wedding ring are further examples. In this kind of buying behaviour consumers are most likely to go through all or most of the stages of the buyer decision process discussed below.

Consumers tend to engage in 'dissonance-reducing buying behaviour' when they are highly involved in the purchase, but have difficulties determining the differences between brands. 'Dissonance' can result from such a purchase if consumers worry afterwards that they may have made the wrong choice. Financial services products, such as insurance or investment products, are good examples. Often a consumer will choose such products on the basis of price or convenience and then seek further confirmation, after the purchase, that they made the right choice. For instance, they may seek out favourable product reviews in newspapers or magazines.

'Habitual buying behaviour' is perhaps the most common type of buying behaviour. This occurs when consumers are not very involved in the purchase, perhaps because the item is bought very frequently and/or does not cost much money, and when they perceive few significant differences between brands. Consumers tend to buy the same brand again and again out of habit, but if their particular brand is not available, or if there is a good offer on a competing brand, they may switch quite easily. Marketers of goods in this category – such as household detergents, soap or toothpaste, many groceries and a large number of other frequently bought items – often use sales and price promotions to entice consumers.

'Well done, another winner, Haskins.'

'Variety-seeking behaviour' occurs when consumers perceive significant differences between brands but are not particularly involved in the purchase. Many groceries fall into this category – for instance, different types of biscuit, bread or ice-cream – where consumers often alternate between different brands for variety.

The buyer decision process

Consumers typically go through a number of stages when making 'complex buying decisions'. These are shown in Figure 3.3.

In the first stage the consumer notices a problem or need which may be solved through purchasing something. A need for financial advice, for example, may be triggered by internal stimuli, such as a large overdraft, or by external stimuli, such as an advertisement by a financial services business or a friend telling you about professional financial advice that helped them.

Figure 3.3 Stages in the buying decision process (Source: Kotler et al., 2001, p. 215, Figure 6.6)

Once the need is felt consumers may search for more information about the products that might satisfy this need. Information search is likely to be very limited or non-existent for habitual and variety-seeking behaviour, but more extensive for complex buying behaviour. Kotler et al. (2001) distinguish between the following information sources:

- *personal sources*: family, friends, neighbours, acquaintances;
- *commercial sources*: advertising, salespeople, the internet, packaging, displays;
- *public sources*: mass media, consumer-rating organisations;
- *experiential sources*: handling, examining, using the product.

While consumers tend to receive the largest quantity of information from commercial sources, the most influential sources are often personal as these are considered more trustworthy; for instance, information received by word of mouth from friends or colleagues. While gathering information about products, consumers already tend to start comparing and evaluating the different products on offer.

Next, the consumer will normally come to a purchase decision. This may be to purchase one of the brands they have looked at. However, consumers may also find that none of the brands fulfils their requirements and that they need to look at an alternative type of product altogether. They may also decide not to purchase a product at this stage. For instance, someone may have a firm intention of buying a new kitchen, but then have their hours at work reduced or face another urgent expenditure. As a result, they may decide to postpone their purchase of the new kitchen.

Consumer behaviour does not stop once a purchase has been made. While using the product they may find that it performs as well or better than they expected, in which case they will be happy with their purchase and may recommend the product to other people. If the product does not perform as well as expected or has faults, however, consumers have a number of options:

- to complain to the seller and expect any faults to be remedied;
- to decide not to buy this kind of product again;
- to tell all their friends and family about the problems they have had with the product.

Businesses need to provide solutions to any post-purchase problems, such as repair or replacement of faulty goods. Businesses are also increasingly asked to take back products at the end of their life span. For instance, the European car industry is being asked to make more car parts recyclable and may be required to take back old cars in the future. At the end of their useful life, products need to be disposed of. This can be a problem for consumers if, for example, the product contains any harmful materials such as the coolants in refrigerators.

Activity 3.1

Spend about **30 minutes** on this activity

Purpose: to link the theory of buying behaviour to your own experience.

Task: think about a recent purchase where you have engaged in complex buying behaviour.

1   Describe the stages in the buying decision process that you went through.

2   How were this process and the final decision you made influenced by elements of the marketing environment?

Feedback

1   The stages you have identified may coincide with those depicted in Figure 3.3, but you may also have skipped some or gone through them in a different order. Your information sources, the brands you considered, the attributes you found important, how the different brands matched your needs and the final decision you made will, of course, depend on the product you were buying, as well as your personal preferences. You should also have thought about what you did with the product after you purchased it, whether there were any problems with it and, if so, what you did about them.

2   Any influences from the marketing environment will also depend on the kind of product you bought and your own circumstances and preferences. You may have identified some sociological and demographic influences, such as your age group, family circumstances or ethnic background; economic influences, such as your income or the general economic outlook; environmental influences, such as a preference for ecologically sound products; technological influences, such as the compatibility of a product with other technological systems that you may use; and/or political influences such as the legality of certain types of products.

Business buying behaviour

When thinking about marketing, people often think first of consumer marketing, but business-to-business marketing is actually equally or even more important. The overall volume of business-to-business markets is much larger than that of consumer markets. There are some differences between consumer and business-to-business markets of which you should be aware. According to Kotler et al. (2001) the most important differences relate to:

- market structure and demand
- the nature of the ***buying unit***
- types of buying behaviour.

In business markets, there are typically fewer but bigger buyers. There are fewer buying businesses than there are consumers, but each business is likely to buy much larger quantities of a product than a single consumer would. For this reason business-to-business marketers tend to rely much more on **personal selling** directly to customers. Often business markets are also more geographically concentrated than consumer markets. In the UK, for instance, many financial services businesses have traditionally been based in London. Businesses buy things that enter the production process which produces consumer goods and services. If demand for consumer goods changes, then demand for raw materials, parts, energy and other things bought by businesses also changes.

'We're going to spend £5M to put over the message that our product is so good it sells itself!'

Business purchases normally involve more people in the decision making. The more complex a purchase is, the more people are likely to be involved in it. For instance, the purchase of a piece of production machinery may involve staff from research and development, the engineering department, the production department, the purchasing department and even, if it is a particularly important purchase, top management. It is important for marketers that sales people can deal knowledgeably with all these staff in the buying unit.

As with consumer behaviour, there are different types of business buying behaviour. The most important of these are:

- *new task*: something a business buys for the first time;
- *straight re-buys*: a simple repeat order for something the business buys regularly: for example, office stationery;
- *modified re-buy*: the business buys something it has bought before but wants some modifications to the new purchase: for example, replacement for worn-out equipment.

A new task is probably the most complex buying situation, particularly if the item needed is highly important to the business process and is expensive. Production machinery or a new IT system may fall into this category. A large number of people tend to be involved in the buying process and lengthy discussions with potential suppliers may be necessary before any decision is made. In straight or modified re-buys the business is more likely to stay with the existing supplier as long as there have been no problems with previous purchases. Often, long-term buyer–supplier relationships develop in these areas.

Activity 3.2

Spend about **15 minutes** on this activity

Purpose: to help you gain a better understanding of the types of buying decisions made by businesses.

Task: imagine that you are setting up a small fashion boutique or sportswear shop (you can use another type of business with which you are more familiar, if you like). Try to answer the following questions:

1   What kinds of products and services does this shop need to buy?

2   Which of these would fall into the 'new task', 'straight re-buy' or 'modified re-buy' categories?

Tip: If you have difficulty imagining the products bought by these kinds of businesses, you could visit one in your area and observe the sorts of things they have and use in the shop. (The activity timing given above obviously doesn't include any store visits.)

Feedback

1   Initially the store will need to be fitted out, with wallpaper, carpets, furniture, cash tills, computer, and so on. One of the biggest recurring purchases will be the stock; that is, fashion items, sportswear. A store like this will also need many other items, such as carrier bags, shoe boxes, hangers, office stationery, cleaning products, etc. Services, such as accounting, marketing research or advertising, or cleaning services, may also be needed.

2   The initial purchases to set up the store (including fitting out and first purchase of everything) are, of course, all new tasks and will be considered carefully. Fittings, furniture and furnishings are particularly important as they will determine the ambience of the shop. Stock purchases will probably always be considered as 'new task' as getting the right fashion or sports items, which will appeal to customers, is crucial to success. After the initial purchase, other items, such as office equipment or hangers, etc., will probably become straight re-buys, if the manager is happy with them, or modified re-buys if small changes are desired.

3.2 Social and cultural aspects of consumption

We will now look at the role of marketing and consumption in the wider social environment. Marketing is not only an aspect of business management; increasingly, it is also seen as an important feature of contemporary, affluent societies (sometimes called consumer societies). We will first look at the notion of 'consumer society' and what this entails. After that we will discuss cultural and social aspects of modern consumption, particular the notions of consumption as hedonistic pleasure, as part of building self-identity and as communication. Understanding the wider context of contemporary consumption is crucial for businesses operating in consumer markets, as consumer behaviour is more complex than a series of marketing inputs and consumer behaviour responses.

Consumer society

Consumption and marketing are important aspects of contemporary affluent societies. McCracken describes consumption as essentially a cultural phenomenon and argues that:

> ... in Western developed societies culture is profoundly connected to and dependent upon consumption. Without consumer goods, modern, developed societies would lose key instruments for the reproduction, representation, and manipulation of their culture ... The meaning of consumer goods ... [is an] important [part] of the scaffolding of our present realities. Without consumer goods, certain acts of self-definition and collective definition in this culture would be impossible.

(McCracken, 1990, p. xi)

Consumer society is characterised by the fact that a large proportion of the population has access to a wide variety of consumer goods. People increasingly define their lifestyle and position in life at least partly through the goods and services that they own and consume. Consumer society has been made possible only by industrialisation, which facilitated the mass production of large numbers of consumer goods and then found a way of making these goods available to the majority of the population. According to Miles (1998), a crucial development in the emergence of consumer society was the growth of working-class purchasing power. What used to be luxury goods (such as dishwashers) gradually became everyday items affordable by the majority of people. This applies only to affluent, industrialised societies, however. In many countries of the so-called developing world even today the vast majority of the population can only dream of possessing consumer goods that we in the industrialised world take for granted. Consumption thus came to play an ever more important role in people's lives and gradually the style and image of consumer goods became as important, if not more so, than their functional value. This was accompanied and encouraged by marketing tools, most notably advertising, which announced the availability of these items to everybody and painted images of glamorous lifestyles using a variety of consumer goods.

As Gabriel and Lang (1995) observe, views on the merits of consumer society are mixed. Some think that the rise of consumer society allows new freedom for people and gives meaning to their lives in an age when religion and political ideologies have lost their meaning for many people. Other views are more critical and argue that consumer society promotes excessive preoccupation with material goods and money. Some commentators are more worried about the *materialism* of consumer culture and the damage done to the natural environment. Kilbourne (1998) argues that contemporary consumer societies value money and material wealth above all else. People

constantly buy new goods rather than continuing to use and perhaps repair old but still serviceable ones. For Kilbourne, these trends are at the heart of the current environmental crisis.

Activity 3.3

Spend about **15 minutes** on this activity

Purpose: to relate the concept of consumer society to your own experience.

Task: try to answer the two questions below:

1 Do you think we live in a consumer society?

2 Can you think of examples where your own lifestyle, status and image might be – partly – defined through consumer goods?

Feedback

If you live in an affluent society, such as Western Europe, you will probably answer the first question with 'yes'. You may have thought about aspects of modern life which remain less touched by consumption, but will probably have found that there are not that many.

Examples of consumer goods that influence our lifestyle, self-image or status are numerous and different people will come up with different instances of this. The music we like to listen to, the clothes we wear, the cars we drive, the kind of holidays we take, to give just a few examples, all contribute to an image of ourselves, our lifestyles and the status we may have in our own and in other people's eyes.

Let us now look at three cultural and social aspects of consumption in greater detail:

1   hedonistic consumption;

2   consumption as a means to construct self-identity;

3   consumption as a means to construct and express social relationships and to communicate social and cultural meaning.

Hedonistic consumption

Most of us are familiar with the idea that consumption can be an activity that brings pleasure. Many people enjoy the act of shopping itself; for instance, the anticipation, the browsing and the comparison of goods, the atmosphere of smart shops or lively markets. Many goods and services, such as holidays or personal grooming products, are bought precisely because they are pleasurable to use. Independent of the actual use we may also gain pleasure from merely owning certain things, because they allow us to show off our style and taste to others (Bourdieu, 1984) or to dream and fantasise about enjoyable, even if often somewhat unrealistic, scenarios involving these objects (Campbell, 1987). For example, the owner of a pair of high-performance running shoes might perhaps dream about running a marathon one day.

Consumption and identity

A second aspect of consumption is the way in which it can become a means to help people construct (and communicate) their psychological identity. At one time, the work you did, the kind of house you lived in, the kind of person you might marry, how you dressed and even the religion to which you adhered were generally more or less determined at birth. In modern societies this has changed. People rarely remain in the place in which they were born but move around. They have far more freedom to choose their work, their partners and their lifestyle. This means that they often need to think about their own identity, and that they can and need to decide on their lifestyle from different options (Giddens, 1991).

Consumption can play a major role in these choices. Through the kind of goods and services that we choose to buy – and those that we don't choose to buy – we say something about ourselves, our preferences, our tastes, our lifestyle and our economic and social status. Not only very special things, but any kind of object may be loaded with meaning and used to build an identity and self-image (Featherstone, 1991; Baudrillard, 1997). In this way, consumers can use products to build an image of who they are and what they believe (Gabriel and Lang, 1995).

Consumption as communication

Many consumption activities take place in social settings, most frequently the family, but also within circles of friends, work groups, and others. Consumption becomes a kind of *language* through which people show their status and taste (Veblen, 1925 [1899]; Bourdieu, 1984), and through which they express social relationships. For instance, Douglas and Isherwood (1978) found that the food people serve and the porcelain, glass and silverware that they use when entertaining guests at home varies depending on whether the guests are parents-in-law, the boss or friends. The chosen type of meal and surroundings make subtle – and sometimes not so subtle – statements about the relationship between host and guests. Can you think of some consumer goods that you own and what (you think that) they say about you?

3.3 Ethical issues in customer relations

Customers are some of the most important stakeholders in a business. For this reason, it is widely accepted that businesses have responsibilities towards their customers. Most businesses realise that it is in their own best interest to treat their customers well. The concept of relationship marketing, in particular, is built on mutual trust that can only develop if both parties behave in a responsible way towards each other. Nonetheless, there are many examples of businesses behaving in unethical ways towards their customers.

At one level it could be argued that customers enter into purchase agreements out of their own free will and that it is up to them to make sure that the products and services they buy meet their requirements. This is known as the *caveat emptor* ('buyer beware') principle. However, this is often not fair to customers, particularly individual consumers. Typically, consumers have less knowledge than producers about products, particularly about the less obvious aspects, such as quality and safety standards or durability. Producers have a knowledge advantage because they concentrate on a range of related products, have technical expertise about the products they sell and may keep important information to themselves. The law in most countries therefore recognises consumers' rights to be truthfully informed about the various aspects of the product and to demand repair, exchange or refunding of unsatisfactory purchases and compensation if a malfunction of a product leads to further damage. But the law does not cover all eventualities, and businesses have a responsibility to keep the justified interests of their customers in mind, even where there are no specific laws.

Example 3.1 illustrates this.

Example 3.1

Guardian Assurance has been fined £750,000 by the City watchdog for 'serious systemic flaws' in its handling of endowment complaints.

The Financial Services Authority (FSA) said that new procedures launched by Guardian Assurance and Guardian Linked Life Assurance Limited (Guardian) in January 2003 were not appropriate or effective in ensuring that complaints from customers were investigated fairly and adequately.

The life and pensions firm, which was bought by the financial services company Aegon in 1999, is now closed to new business.

The FSA said that in the period until December 2004, 5,600 customers whose complaints were rejected by the firm had been exposed to the risk of financial loss.

Following the introduction of the new system, the FSA claimed, the number of complaints upheld by the insurer dropped significantly, from 71% in the second half of 2002 to 22.6% in the first half of 2003.

From April 2003 there was also a significant increase in the proportion of complaints rejected by the firm but subsequently upheld by the Financial Ombudsman Service (FOS).

According to the FSA, Guardian was aware in advance that the changes it was making would significantly reduce the number of complaints it upheld.

…

'Guardian failed to treat its customers fairly by exposing those with a valid complaint to the risk that their complaint could be rejected inappropriately,' said Margaret Cole, the FSA's director of enforcement. 'Consequently, they may not have received the compensation to which they were entitled. …'

The watchdog said problems had only come to light during a visit by the FSA to the firm in late 2004, made as part of its work with the endowment industry on complaints handling.

…

Guardian is not the first endowment provider to be fined for failures in its handling of customer complaints and its fine is roughly in line with others handed out.

In December 2003, the FSA fined Friends Provident Life and Pensions £675,000, in March 2004 Allied Dunbar Assurance was fined £725,000 and last year Abbey National received a £800,000 fine.

…

The Financial Services Ombudsman said today that it expected to handle a record number of complaints in 2006 as increasing numbers of people contacted it about endowment mis-selling. The service predicted

> it would see a 28% rise in the number of complaints it resolved in the first three months of this year and that it expected to settle a record 125,000 cases in the coming financial year.
>
> However it predicted that the volume of endowment complaints is likely to have peaked by March 2007.
>
> (Source: *Guardian*, 2006)

Marketers' responsibilities towards their customers arise across all aspects of marketing, including product policy, marketing communications, pricing, distribution, marketing strategy and market research. Essential Reading 3, which you read for the next activity, discusses some of these issues in more detail.

Activity 3.4

Spend about **1 hour** on this activity

Purpose: to consolidate your understanding of the aspects of marketing ethics.

Task: read Essential Reading 3, 'Consumers and business ethics' by Andrew Crane and Dirk Matten, which you will find at the back of this book. This should take about 30 of the 60 minutes suggested for this activity. Choose one of the examples of unethical marketing practice given by Crane and Matten and answer the following questions:

1   Why is this practice unethical?

2   Does it violate consumer rights? If so, how?

3   Could you argue that consumers should have paid more attention to avoid damage to themselves from the marketing practice?

Feedback

To take the first example, of tobacco marketing:

1   This is considered unethical because tobacco companies have used advertising to paint a glamorous picture of smoking while withholding evidence that the nicotine contained in tobacco is addictive.

2   It can be argued that the tobacco companies violated consumers' rights by treating them merely as a means to earning profits without caring about the damage to health that smoking caused.

3   You might well argue that the health-damaging consequences of tobacco are well known today and consumers only have themselves to blame if they become ill from smoking. In the past, however, it was claimed that the tobacco companies had known about the health-damaging properties of tobacco long before the general public and had even suppressed that information in order to maintain tobacco sales.

As always, you should refer to the appropriate part of your Study Companion for extra reflection and learning on this and other activities throughout this book.

3.4 Conclusion

In this study session you have learnt more about customers and their behaviour. Businesses need to understand customer behaviour in order to market their products effectively. You have learnt to distinguish between different types of consumer behaviour and between consumer and business buying behaviour. You have also learnt about the contrast between a rational, individualistic view of consumption and a conception of consumption as a social and cultural activity. Finally, you have considered ethical issues in businesses' dealings with their customers. In the next study session we will look at the way in which businesses adjust the elements of the marketing mix to position themselves favourably in customers' minds.

3.5 Learning outcomes

By the end of this study session on understanding customers and consumption you should be able to:

- differentiate between different types of buyer behaviour;
- explain complex buying decision processes;
- discuss differences between consumer and business buying behaviour;
- contrast a rational approach to understanding customers with a social and cultural understanding of consumption;
- explain three main aspects of cultural and social functions of consumption.
- You will have developed your learning by:
- reflecting on an example of ethical issues in marketing financial services (Example 3.1);
- reading the abridged book chapter (Essential Reading 3) by Andrew Crane and Dirk Matten and discussing an example of unethical marketing practice.

Session 4 The marketing mix

Why are we studying 'the marketing mix'? Marketing is more than just a set of techniques employed by marketing managers. However, these techniques are important in that marketers must try to design an offering which will appeal to customers. This offering is the marketing mix.

The **aims and objectives** of Session 4 are to:

- explain the concept and the elements of the marketing mix;
- contrast different types of products, including physical goods and services;
- explain the key features of the product life cycle and new product development;
- contrast different approaches to pricing and explain some typical methods of pricing for strategic effect;
- explain distribution channels and who their members are;
- explain the different elements of marketing communications and how they are commonly used;
- consider some common ethical issues related to elements of the marketing mix;
- explain why services marketing is different from goods marketing and introduce the extended marketing mix for services.

4.1 Products

Products can be described as a 'bundle of benefits'. This means that it is not usually the actual product itself which is important to customers but what it will do for them. For instance, if you buy a mobile phone you may be really buying a means of staying in touch with friends, family, business partners and others. This is the reason why physical products cannot only be substituted by other physical products but also by services that perform the same function. Instead of buying a car you might decide to use taxi rides or become a member of a car share pool.

There are three levels of product benefits. The core benefit is the kind of main benefit described above; for example, communicating with friends and family in the case of a mobile phone. The actual product has product features and characteristics in addition to the core benefit. These distinguish one brand from another. All mobile phones serve as means of communication, but actual mobile phones also have various other features, ranging from additional functions such as internet access, games or picture messaging to the shape and colour of the casing. At the third level, augmented product benefits may include after-sales services, such as an answering service in the case of mobile phones, free warranties if something goes wrong with the phone or the option to upgrade to the latest version at a lower price. The three levels of product benefits are illustrated in Figure 4.1.

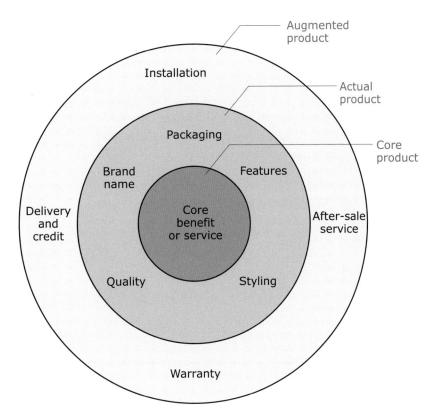

Figure 4.1 Three levels of product (Source: Kotler et al., 2001, p. 460, Figure 13.1)

Physical goods and services are both products and in many respects they are bought and sold in similar ways. Physical goods are generally thought of as tangible, and services as intangible. Nearly all physical goods have some intangible elements, however, such as advice given before the customer buys something, delivery and instalment, and after-sales services, such as repairs. Likewise, most services include some tangible goods, such as the food served in a restaurant or the hair care products applied by a hair stylist. It is therefore best to think of a continuum of products, ranging from nearly entirely tangible at one extreme to nearly entirely intangible at the other extreme, with various combinations of tangible and intangible between these two poles. This is illustrated in Figure 4.2.

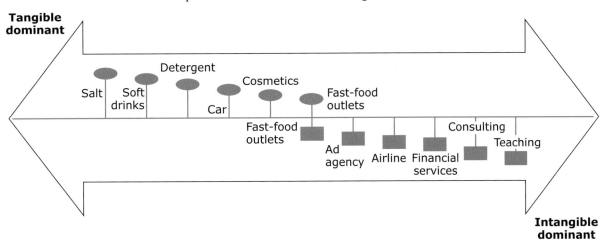

Figure 4.2 Tangible and intangible continuum for goods and services (Source: Kotler et al., 2001, p. 536, Figure 15.1)

The product life cycle

Products generally go through a life cycle. This means that they are launched at some point and after a time of growth and maturity they eventually decline and become obsolete. This life cycle is reflected in the level of sales and profits across time and can be plotted on a two-dimensional curve, as depicted in Figure 4.3.

Figure 4.3 Product life cycle (Source: Blythe, 2001, p. 103, Figure 6.2)

We can think of the product life cycle as having five phases: product development, introduction, growth, maturity and eventual decline. After a new product has been developed and is first introduced to the market, sales may grow quite slowly initially as not many people yet know about it. As it becomes better known, sales may grow quite rapidly until they tend to level off during the maturity phase, when many potential target customers have already bought it and more competitors introduce similar products. Thus, eventually the sales of many products decline as most customers already have them (the market is saturated) and new substitute products are introduced. Decline is, however, not inevitable as there are many strategies by which businesses can extend the life of their products. The life cycle concept is useful for describing what is happening to a product at a particular moment but it is not much use for predicting the product's future.

A life cycle curve may be drawn up for a product category, such as hair care products; for an actual product type, such as leave-in-conditioner; and for individual brands within that product type. The life cycles of product categories tend to be longer than those of actual product types and the life cycles of brands are often the shortest, but this can vary considerably. The life cycles of some brands can span many decades and even centuries (Persil washing powder was launched in the nineteenth century), whereas some 'fad' products have very short life cycles (for example, Rubik's Cube).

New product development

Although the death of existing products is not inevitable, the concept of the product life cycle suggests that most products will eventually decline. This is a powerful reason why businesses constantly strive to develop new products. The process of creating new products is more of an art than an exact science and it is difficult to generalise about it. However, a frequently quoted model of the new product development process was proposed by Crawford (1991). In this model, a number of steps of new product development are shown in the following sequence:

1 *New product planning* A business looks at its current products, how well they are performing, and where the marketing environment poses threats to existing products and opportunities for new products.

2 *Idea generation* Specific ideas for new products are generated and collected, perhaps through group discussion techniques such as brainstorming.

3 *Idea screening and evaluation* The ideas generated in the previous step are examined for their feasibility and marketability.

4 *Technical development* The technical aspects of the product are investigated and a prototype is developed.

5 *Market appraisal* Market research is carried out to assess whether the product would be successful in the market.

6 *Launch* The product is produced and offered in the market.

Although most businesses are likely to cover all these stages in some form, they may not give the same priority to each stage and may not follow a strict sequence. The businesses most successful at developing new products often carry out several of these stages simultaneously. For example, during the 1980s and 1990s it was thought that Japanese car makers were much better at bringing out new models quickly because they were able to shorten the new product development process by doing several steps at the same time. Some businesses are much better at developing new products than others and this may be because of their organisational culture, which values innovativeness and does not kill off new ideas too quickly. This is illustrated in Example 4.1 on innovation at 3M.

Example 4.1

3M: company background

The Minnesota Mining & Manufacturing Corporation (3M) is well known for its capacity to innovate. Some of its best-known brands are Scotch tapes, Scotch-Brite cleaning products and Post-it notes. In 2000 nearly 35 per cent of its total sales came from products that had been introduced within the previous four years. More than 75,000 3M employees create more than 500 new products every year.

3M prides itself on a corporate culture that promotes entrepreneurship. Early in 3M's history, chair and chief executive officer (CEO) William L. McKnight introduced policies that were thought responsible for 3M's ability to innovate. These policies and philosophies (shown below) are still being expanded as management believes innovation to be the main factor in 3M's future success.

Policies for innovation at 3M

'15 Percent Option' Many employees have the option to spend up to 15 per cent of their work on individual projects of their own choice. They need not disclose or justify the project to a manager.

'30 Percent Rule' Thirty per cent of business unit revenues must come from products introduced in the last four years.

Career paths The technical career ladder offers equal advancement opportunities to the management career ladder. This enables employees to stay focused on their research and professional interests if they wish.

Seed capital Seed capital to develop new product ideas can be requested from employees' own business units, any other business unit within 3M or the corporate office. After obtaining seed capital, the employee assembles a team to develop the product.

Tolerance for failure If the innovation does not succeed, the team members are guaranteed their previous jobs. Company culture emphasises that a failure can turn into a success; there is no punishment for a product failing in the market.

Rewards for success As the venture achieves certain revenue goals, the team members receive pay rises, promotions and recognition.

(Sources: based on Collins and Porras, 1995; Mitsch, 1990)

Activity 4.1

Spend about **45 minutes** on this activity

Purpose: to help you understand the factors that may make a business successful in product innovation.

Task: read Example 4.1 on 3M again. Make notes on the following questions:

1   How do you think 3M's culture of innovation differs from the culture of other businesses that may be less innovative?

2   Why do you think it is important for 3M to give employees some free time to work on innovation projects as they choose, without explanation or justification?

3   Why do you think 3M tolerates failure in product innovation?

Feedback

1   3M is unusual in allowing employees time of their own to explore new product ideas without any need for justification or even explanation. Many businesses try to control employees' use of working time much more tightly than this. An explicit goal of 30 per cent of revenue from new products is also ambitious and unusual and so is the variety of funding opportunities for new products. Note, however, that still not all new product ideas are likely to be funded. Many businesses proclaim that they encourage experimentation and tolerate failure, but in practice this is often not the case.

2   If employees need to justify new product projects in advance, innovative
    ideas may be discarded straight away as too risky or too off-beat. Truly
    innovative ideas often seem highly unorthodox at the start and their
    potential may only become clear once someone has put some effort into
    thinking them through.

3   If failure is punished people will become risk averse and not pursue risky
    but potentially very productive ideas. A large proportion of new products
    fail in the market but if businesses were to let that discourage them there
    would be no product innovation at all. Also, failed product ideas can
    sometimes still become successful if applied differently. For instance, 3M's
    well-known Post-it notes started out as a failed project to produce a new
    adhesive, which was found to be too weak for its intended purpose but
    turned out to be ideal for the Post-it notes.

Although some form of new product development is highly important to
most businesses and many put considerable resources and expertise into their
new product development processes, new products often fail in the market.
Not all innovations which seem technically brilliant to the experts really
fulfil a need in the market. For instance, picture messaging in mobile phone
technology got off to a slow start because many consumers did not really see
the need to send each other pictures via the phone. On the other hand, heavy
reliance on market research in the early product development stages may
also lead to less than successful innovation. Consumers generally find it very
difficult to envisage real technological innovations and tend to think in terms
of slight improvements to existing products. If businesses rely heavily on
consumer feedback to suggest new products they may end up being rather
timid in their innovation strategies.

4.2 Pricing

Pricing is one of the most important issues for businesses. It is of crucial
importance for the quantity of product being sold and for the profits made.
The difference between getting the price right and getting it wrong can be
the difference between being successful and going out of business.

Approaches to pricing

The key problem for businesses is to decide what price will be considered as
good value for money by customers while allowing the business to make a
satisfactory profit. There are three main approaches to setting prices, which
vary in the degree to which they are customer oriented (Blythe, 2001):

1   cost-based pricing

2   customer-based pricing

3   competition-based pricing.

Cost-based pricing is the least customer-oriented pricing method and is thus
not entirely compatible with a marketing orientation. It is, however, used by
many businesses as costs are relatively easy to work out and these pricing

methods are therefore more straightforward than customer-based pricing. It works by adding up all the costs of manufacturing and selling a product and then adding a fixed profit percentage.

Customer-based pricing is more in line with a marketing orientation as it starts with the customer's willingness to pay. It does not necessarily mean offering the product at the lowest possible price, but at a price that the customer considers 'good value', taking into account quality and other product features. Customer-based pricing is more complex to carry out as good estimates of customers' perceptions of value and willingness to pay need to be made.

Competition-based pricing involves comparing the prices of all competing products and then setting the price of one's own product. This may be lower than the competition if the business is competing on price. It may also be more expensive than the competition if the business is competing on quality, style or some other product features and wants to express the superiority of its products through the price. In practice, businesses will take into account all three elements of costs, customer perceptions and competition when setting prices.

Pricing for strategic effect

Pricing also includes decisions on discounts and price differentiation, as well as relative prices for the whole product range. 'Product line pricing' refers to the setting of prices within linked product groups. Sometimes sales of one product are directly linked to sales of another product. It may therefore be possible to sell one product cheaply in order to encourage more purchases of another product and thus achieve a higher sales volume. For instance, the sales of game consoles and games are closely linked. By selling consoles cheaply, marketers may encourage more people to buy them. These people will then also start buying games, which may be priced more highly.

'Psychological pricing' involves setting prices in such a way that they capture or encourage particular psychological effects in consumers. High prices do not always discourage consumers from buying a product and some products actually sell better if priced highly than if priced cheaply. For example, a maker of luxury watches will probably be more successful if these are sold at a substantial price as the high price in itself will suggest luxury and status. Buyers of such watches feel that they own something which not everybody can afford and that can give them a sense of status.

Ethical issues in pricing

Pricing is an area of the marketing mix where irresponsible and unethical actions are often found (Crane and Matten, 2004). In a *market economy* prices are, in principle, negotiated depending on supply and demand but, because of the power differences that often exist between producers and consumers, there is room for unethical pricing practice. Producers of fashion or entertainment goods, for example, are often accused of charging excessive prices for goods that may be much cheaper to produce. They can do this because competing businesses may agree that they will all charge the higher price. This is generally illegal but often difficult to prove.

Predatory pricing is another unethical pricing tactic. Here, a business offers its products at artificially low prices, below the cost of production, with the aim of winning a majority of customers and driving competitors out of the market. Consumers only benefit temporarily from such a practice as the business will later put up prices after the competition has been weakened or eliminated.

4.3 Distribution

The third element in the marketing mix is the distribution channel (relating to the 'place' where the product is sold). Producing an attractive product and pricing it so that it gives good value is only part of the story. It must also be available in a place where customers can find and buy it.

Distribution channels are the channels by which products are made available to their final customers. At one level this relates to the physical transportation and storage of goods. However, distribution channels do much more than just transporting and storing goods. They also transfer ownership of the goods, offer advice to customers and provide after-sales services.

An example of competitive pricing

Members of the distribution channel

Some distribution channels are very short; that is, they have few members, whereas others are long and have many members. The shortest distribution channels are those in which producers sell directly to final customers without any intermediaries. For instance, farmers might sell vegetables, meat and eggs directly to consumers through a farm shop on their own premises; many industrial products are sold directly from manufacturer to customers without any intermediaries; many businesses sell directly to consumers by mail order; and the internet now plays an important role in connecting businesses directly with their customers without the need for further intermediaries.

Slightly longer are those channels which include retailers as well as producers and final customers. Distribution channels involving large retail businesses often take this shape. Large retail chains are able to buy directly from the manufacturers most of the goods they sell because they have the financial ability to buy large quantities and the logistical capability to store them and distribute them around the country to their own stores.

Smaller retailers, on the other hand, are often not in a position to buy directly from manufacturers. In this case the channel contains a further level, namely wholesalers. These are businesses that buy large quantities directly from manufacturers and sell on smaller quantities to smaller stores, such as small, local grocery stores.

Sometimes even wholesalers are not in direct contact with producers. In this case, a broker or agent may act as an additional intermediary between producers and wholesalers. This is often the case in international marketing situations where neither the producer nor the wholesaler is large enough to deal directly with a business in a different country, or where the amount sold is too small to warrant wholesalers or producers going to the effort of dealing directly with each other. Table 4.1 summarises the different lengths of distribution channels.

Table 4.1 Distribution channels

Channel 1	Manufacturer				Consumer
Channel 2	Manufacturer			Retailer	Consumer
Channel 3	Manufacturer		Wholesaler	Retailer	Consumer
Channel 4	Manufacturer	Other intermediary	Wholesaler	Retailer	Consumer

(Source: adapted from Kotler et al., 2001, p. 742)

Wholesalers are businesses that buy products from producers and sell them on to retailers. They often carry out a number of functions in the distribution channel, such as storage and transportation, information gathering and dissemination, or certain promotional activities, which otherwise would have to be carried out by individual manufacturers or retailers. By carrying out these tasks on behalf of manufacturers and retailers, wholesalers can achieve economies of scale and improve the efficiency of the whole distribution channel.

Retailers are businesses that buy from producers or wholesalers and sell on to consumers. When we think of retailers we typically think of high street shops or out-of-town superstores, but there are other types of retailers, such as mail-order catalogue businesses, internet sellers or even door-to-door salespeople. In recent years, the internet has become a very important place where businesses and their customers meet. Many businesses sell direct from their websites to consumers, but internet retailers are also very important. Well-known examples include internet travel agents such as Expedia, or booksellers such as Amazon. If you have not used any online shopping websites you may like to look at one now, at the end of this study session or when you have finished this book. Type the name of a favourite retailer into an internet search engine, such as Yahoo! or Google.

Successful retailing is thought to depend on a number of factors, including:

- the convenient location of a store;
- the right kind of goods offered in the right quantities (the product mix);
- the right level of service for the type of good and outlet;
- the image of the store;
- the atmosphere and ambience of the shop.

Increasingly, retailers are relying on information technology to collect information on their customers and to make tailored offers to them. Loyalty cards or discount schemes are frequently used means of gaining more information about customers' preferences, as well as encouraging them to spend more money at a particular retail store.

4.4 Marketing communications

Marketing communications is not a straight forward, one-way process from marketers to potential customers. As in any communication process, both the sender of a message and the receiver of that message (for instance, speaker and listener) are actively involved. If one person is speaking to another and that other person is distracted and not listening, no communication occurs. Likewise, if the sounds the speaker makes are drowned out by loud background noise, even if the other person is trying to listen, they will at best receive the message very incompletely and again no real communication occurs. It is also possible that the speaker is speaking clearly, the listener is listening carefully, and there are no distractions and no background noise, but the listener interprets what is being said in a very different way from the meaning the speaker intends. Let's assume I have agreed with my partner to go for a walk on Sunday morning. On that morning the sky is cloudy and it looks as though it might start to rain. I might say, 'It looks like it's about to rain,' meaning to say that we should take raincoats on our walk, but my partner might interpret my sentence as meaning that I don't want to go. We have not communicated properly.

Similar problems arise in marketing communications. They are further compounded by the fact that in many types of marketing communication there is no direct contact between the sender and the receiver of a message. Instead, the message is sent through a medium, as in the case of advertising or publicity, or is built into a display or pricing information, as may be the case in sales promotions. Additionally, marketing messages are now so numerous that potential customers often pay very little or no attention to any particular message. In fact, they may actively try to avoid or ignore marketing communications, for instance by changing television channels during advertising breaks or by refusing to listen to salespeople either at the door or on the telephone.

Marketing communications are often expensive for businesses. In order to make sure that money is spent in the most effective and efficient way and that the intended message has the greatest possible chance of being received by its intended audience, businesses often make great efforts to plan their communications carefully.

Marketers often follow the so-called AIDA approach, which suggests that good marketing communication should go through the sequence of stimulating 'awareness', 'interest', 'desire' and 'action' on the part of consumers. Not every single communication action will be directed at each of these stages, although when a business launches a new product it must first make consumers aware of the product. If the product is highly innovative this may be done through public relations, by securing a write-up in a specialist magazine or even in a general magazine or newspaper, as well as advertising. Awareness may lead to interest on the part of the consumer, but further advertising, or perhaps promotions in the form of free samples, may increase interest levels. Once a level of awareness and interest has been stimulated, marketers may concentrate on trying to raise consumers' desire for the product; for instance, through advertising that focuses on the situations in which the product might be used or on the social status it could confer. Action, in the form of a first trial, can be stimulated by free samples, money-off vouchers or similar sales promotion techniques.

We will now look in turn at the different elements of marketing communications, also sometimes called the promotional mix. The promotional mix consists of advertising, sales promotions, personal selling and public relations. Depending on the kind of business, product and market, a business may focus on different elements of the mix. However, few businesses will use one form of marketing communication exclusively; nor are the different elements necessarily substitutes for each other. Each element has different strengths and weaknesses and they are generally used in some combination that best reflects the particular communications needs of the business at a particular time. It should also be noted that marketing communications are not always directed at customers. They can also be aimed at employees, pressure groups and other stakeholders in the business. Figure 4.4 summarises the type of messages and the type of audience for which the different elements of the promotional mix are suitable.

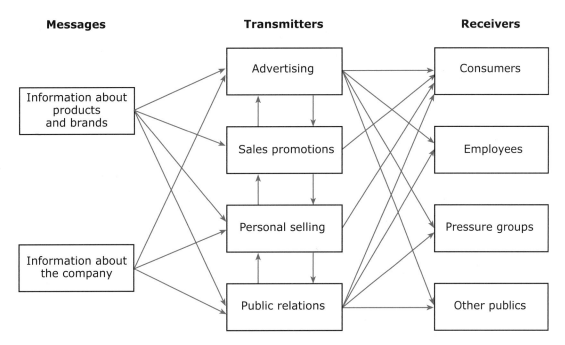

Figure 4.4 The promotional mix (Source: Blythe, 2001, p. 175, Figure 9.3)

Advertising

Unlike some other elements in the promotional mix, advertising is impersonal and communicates with a large number of people through a paid media channel. There are different types of advertising (Brassington and Pettitt, 2005). Pioneering advertising is used in the early stages of the product life cycle, when businesses want to achieve consumer awareness and interest. Competitive advertising may be more appropriate at a later stage in the product life cycle, when it is necessary for businesses to distinguish their product from those offered by competitors. Comparative advertising, which directly compares the benefits of a brand against those of its leading competitors, is one form of competitive advertising. Reminder or reinforcement advertising is designed to operate after consumers have already purchased the product. It serves to reassure them of the product's benefits and to confirm that they made the right choice in selecting this particular product and brand.

Another type of advertising attempts to improve the general reputation and image of the organisation. It is often directed at a whole range of stakeholders, including local government, community, and pressure groups. Through this the organisation tries to build up general goodwill in the community.

Sales promotions

'Sales promotions' refers to the specific element of the promotional mix which tries to create a temporary increase in sales by offering customers an incentive to buy the product. Within this general definition, sales promotions come in many different forms. Brassington and Pettitt (2005) distinguish between the following types of sales promotion techniques:

- *Money based* Easy to implement, very common (but therefore doesn't generate much excitement), can give money back to people who would have bought anyway, expensive:

  - cash-back (collect tokens to get refund)

  - immediate price reductions at point of sale

  - coupons.

- *Product based* Less likely to 'cheapen' product image:

  - 'X % extra free'

  - 'buy one get one free'

  - free samples

  - piggy-backing with another product: for example, putting a free pack of coffee whitener with a pack of instant coffee.

- *Gift, prize or merchandise based*

  - gifts in return for proof of purchase (toy received on presentation of a certain number of labels from a product)

  - loyalty schemes

  - competitions or sweepstakes (buying a product entitles you to enter a prize draw).

Sales promotions are often used for lower value items. (If they were used for premium or luxury brands they might 'cheapen' the brand image in consumers' eyes.) They tend to work best as part of an integrated communications campaign, where advertising or public relations build the brand image and sales promotions encourage people to try the product or otherwise boost short-term sales.

Personal selling

Personal selling can be a very powerful means of marketing communication, perhaps the most powerful a business has at its disposal. A salesperson who talks personally to a potential customer, finds out about their needs and can explain the benefits of the product is more likely to be successful in making a sale than any advertising, sales promotion or public relations that the business could use instead. Customers also have the opportunity to ask direct questions about the product. However, a sales force also tends to be the most expensive marketing communications tool for a business. Personal selling is therefore mostly used for expensive or highly technical products that need a lengthy decision-making process.

Public relations

Public relations – or PR – is about creating a favourable image for the business in the minds of its stakeholders. It often involves creating and placing favourable news stories. Unlike advertising it is not paid for, but newspapers or other media print present the story if they think it is of sufficient interest to their audience. This also means that the journalists publicising the story have the freedom to present it in their own way and put their own slant on it.

Public relations operate by a number of key routes, including word-of-mouth, press and television news stories, and personal recommendation. It aims to put a positive image of the business and its products into people's minds and conversations. Good PR can be more effective than advertising as it is free and thus saves on the promotional budget; it is often more credible in the eyes of consumers and it is more likely to be read or viewed as it is considered news rather than advertising.

Ethical issues in marketing communications

Marketing communications has the potential to be particularly problematic and marketers have been criticised for a great number of irresponsible and unethical practices in this area (Smith and Quelch, 1993). Perhaps the most obvious issue here is that marketers should not deceive potential customers or make misleading claims about any aspects of the marketing mix. This includes not only claims made through advertising, but also those made through other forms of communication. For instance, overly large and elaborate packaging may give the impression of a larger quantity of the product than the buyer is actually getting and is therefore misleading.

Other criticisms of contemporary marketing communications are that they are often very intrusive and that consumers find it difficult to avoid them; for instance, in the case of internet pop-up advertisements or unsolicited telesales (Smith and Quelch, 1993). On a broader, societal scale, marketing communications have been criticised for creating artificial wants and reinforcing materialistic values. It is claimed by critics that they create insecurity and perpetual dissatisfaction (Crane and Matten, 2004); for instance, by suggesting to people that they should be ashamed of their old mobile phone or by presenting a glorified, unattainable lifestyle, which will leave people unhappy with the lifestyle they have. Marketing communications have also often been criticised for perpetuating social stereotypes; for instance, by portraying only beautiful, slim people as being desirable. Activity 4.2 invites you to think of some examples of unethical advertising.

___

Activity 4.2

Spend about **10 minutes** on this activity

Purpose: to relate the notion of unethical advertising to your own experience.

Task: please think of, or have a look for, an advertisement that you perceive as unethical. Jot down some notes on what it is that you find unethical about this advertisement.

Feedback

In the UK, unethical advertising is controlled by the Advertising Standards Authority. Similar bodies to ensure ethical standards in advertising exist in other countries. However, many advertisements still fall foul of the ethical standards of many people.

Examples of advertisements considered unethical may be those portraying women in revealing or exploitative attire and poses, those for junk food aimed at children, those for products that are very environmentally polluting, and many more.

The above examples would be considered unethical by many because they perpetuate sexual stereotypes and are demeaning to women, encourage overeating and thus childhood obesity, and encourage behaviour that degrades the environment, respectively.

4.5 Marketing services

The idea of the marketing mix was originally developed for physical goods. Services are different from physical goods in a number of ways (Kotler et al., 2001): they are mostly intangible, they are produced and consumed at the same time, their quality varies depending on the person providing the service, and they cannot be produced in advance and stored for later sale or use.

This makes it difficult for customers to assess service quality before buying; for instance, by handling or testing the product. It has, therefore, been suggested that the marketing mix should be extended by further elements, to take better account of the particular nature of services marketing. These elements are the 'people' who deliver the service, the 'processes' by which the service is delivered and any other 'physical evidence' for service quality that the marketer may provide.

Not all services are delivered by people in a face-to-face transaction. Automatic cash machines and vending machines are two examples of services for which the providers are not in face-to-face contact with the customer. In many other cases, however, service quality can vary significantly depending on the person who performs the service and it is often extremely important to customers that they can trust that person. This is particularly true for services that rely on special expertise, such as the services provided by doctors or lawyers. Consumers' satisfaction with, for example, a hair cut or a restaurant meal also depends on the skills of the hairdresser or the chef, respectively. Service providers therefore often place great importance on the attitude and training of their staff.

Consumers can also gain confidence from the processes by which a service is delivered. Restaurant food tastes better and is more wholesome if there are proper processes to make sure that food is fresh and expertly cooked. Whether medical treatment will help a patient depends on the doctor using the correct procedures of diagnosis and treatment. Customers tend to be reassured if those parts of the process that they can see look correct and efficient to them.

Finally, service providers can often provide some kind of physical evidence to suggest that an otherwise intangible service is of good quality. These are the tangible elements of the service. The premises where a service is performed can be an important clue. A clean restaurant seating area gives customers hope that attention is being paid to hygiene, and the quality of the furniture, cutlery and crockery may give an idea of the standard of cooking.

Similarly, customers usually have a fairly clear idea of how they expect the premises of a bank or a doctor's surgery to look and if actual premises do not conform to those expectations they may lose confidence.

Activity 4.3

Spend about **1 hour** on this activity

Purpose: to relate the theory of the marketing mix for services to an actual service situation that you have encountered.

Task: in the next day or two visit the premises of a service provider (perhaps while using their services as part of your normal routine). The hour suggested for this activity does not include the time spent visiting a service provider. After your visit, reflect on the following questions:

1 Would you describe the service as being people based? If so, why and how is it people based?

2 If you think that it is people based, do the people providing the service give an impression of quality service provision? If so, how do they do this? If not, why not?

3 What are the (observable) processes by which the service is provided?

4 Do these processes give the impression of quality service provision? If so, how do they do this? If not, why not?

5 Is there any physical evidence of the quality of the service?

6 If so, what is it and what impression of service quality does it give you?

Feedback

As with many activities, your answers will obviously depend on the service you have chosen. This might be a store-based service, such as a restaurant meal, or a visit to your bank.

1 Store-based services are more likely to be people based than internet services. However, this is not always true. Many banking services can now be delivered through cash and other machines and some internet travel services, for example, allow you to get advice from and book through a particular person.

2 Your impression of service quality also depends on the particular service you choose and your personal preferences, but friendliness, promptness of service, knowledge displayed and a professional manner are often taken as signs of a good service.

3 Processes in a restaurant may involve being greeted and seated at the start, being given a menu and asked for drinks orders, placing an order, being served, and so on.

4 The sequence, completeness, timeliness, and so on, of these steps in the service process all contribute to our perception of service quality.

5 Physical evidence varies significantly between different services. For instance, there will be more physical evidence in a restaurant (premises, furnishings, cutlery and crockery, menu, the actual food, etc.) than in any internet service (but the latter may provide some evidence in the form of pictures and printed receipts, etc.)

6   The quality, appropriateness, quantity, and so on, of physical evidence
can all contribute to our impression of service quality.

4.6 Conclusion

In this study session we have discussed the elements of the marketing mix:
product, price, distribution and marketing communications. You have learnt
about the product life cycle and the importance of new product development.
Different approaches to pricing, different distribution channels and their
members, and the various elements of marketing communications, have been
introduced. You have also learnt about some of the differences between
physical products and services and how the marketing mix can be extended
to be more suitable for marketing services.

Marketing communications are the final but by no means least important
element of the marketing mix. In the next study session we will consider the
way in which marketers have attempted to take on board the societal and
environmental concerns that have been discussed in earlier study sessions.

4.7 Learning outcomes

By the end of this study session on the marketing mix you should be able
to:

- describe the different elements of the marketing mix;
- begin to discuss how a product's performance and marketing
  mix strategies may change over the course of the product life
  cycle;
- start to appreciate the importance and difficulties of product innovation;
- explain some common approaches to pricing;
- describe some common forms of distribution channels and the nature of
  some key channel members;
- discuss the different elements of marketing communication and how they
  are normally used;
- explain the differences between tangible products and services and
  discuss how services marketing differs from the marketing of tangible
  goods;
- discuss some common ethical problems associated with different aspects
  of the marketing mix.

You will have developed your learning by:

- studying an example of product innovation and discussing some key
  aspects of it;
- carrying out a number of further activities to relate concepts to practical
  situations.

Session 5 Addressing societal and environmental concerns in marketing

Why are we studying how businesses address 'societal and environmental concerns in marketing'? Businesses may gain benefits from being seen as socially and environmentally responsible. Consumers may prefer their products, insurance companies may be happier to cover them, or government agencies or pressure groups may be willing to work with them on certain projects. On the other hand, stakeholders may take action against those businesses that they perceive to be contravening standards.

The **aims and objectives** of Session 5 are to:

- define the societal marketing concept and outline how it is used to address common social and ethical concerns with marketing practice;

- introduce the notion of 'green' marketing;

- explore the extent to which 'green' marketing practice addresses environmental concerns with marketing.

5.1 The societal marketing concept

The societal marketing concept can be regarded as an extension of the marketing orientation, discussed in section 1.1 of study Session 1. According to Kotler et al. (2001) the societal marketing concept holds that a business should work out what the needs, wants and expectations of its target customers and markets are. It should then satisfy these needs, wants and expectations better and more efficiently than competing businesses, in a way (and here lies the crucial difference with the marketing orientation) that maintains or improves the consumer's and society's well-being.

Why do we need a societal marketing concept? Kotler et al. (2001) argue that a pure marketing orientation may overlook the fact that what consumers want in the short term and what is good for them in the long term is not necessarily the same. For example, many of us find fast food, such as hamburgers, tasty and consume it frequently, but fast food is often not good for us in the long run, as it can be high in fat and low in fibre and essential nutrients. There can also be conflict between what individual consumers desire and what is good either for society at large or for the environment. Transport is a good example. Most of us enjoy the convenience of travelling by car and/or aeroplane, with the result that the number of cars on our roads and the number of air miles travelled each year have increased enormously over recent years. You will probably be aware of the negative consequences of increased travel, such as air pollution and global warming, congested roads and noise from airports.

Kotler (1972), who was among the first to write about the idea of societal marketing, argued that businesses should think of the products they offered and were developing in terms of two dimensions:

1 the immediate satisfaction they provided to consumers;

2 the long-term consumer welfare they provided.

Figure 5.1 shows four different types of product, depending on whether the score is high or low on these two dimensions.

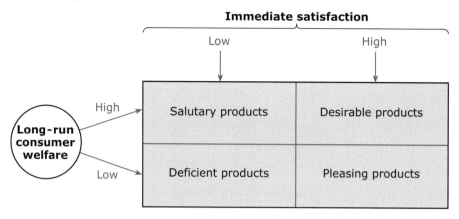

Figure 5.1 Classification of new product opportunities (Source: Kotler, 1972, p. 56, Exhibit II)

To some extent, these four categories are self-explanatory. Kotler suggests that marketing deficient products will not be successful for businesses, as there will be no market for them. Salutary products pose no moral problem but may be difficult to market if consumers derive no immediate satisfaction from them. Many businesses market pleasing products, for which there tends to be a ready market. However, these are precisely the products that, under the societal marketing concept, businesses should not market as they are to the long-term detriment of consumer and societal welfare. Desirable products are just that: desirable for the individual consumer, desirable from a long-term societal perspective and desirable for the business, which should be able to sell these well, and with a good conscience.

The societal and environmental implications of marketing began to be discussed extensively in the late 1960s and 1970s. Many of the concerns raised then are still valid today. Essential Reading 4 is an abridged version of a seminal article from that time. It sets out the key problems of counterbalancing individual choice and societal and individual welfare.

Activity 5.1

Spend about **90 minutes** on this activity

Purpose: to further your understanding of the societal and environmental implications of marketing.

Task: read Essential Reading 4, 'Societal adaptation: a new challenge for marketing' by Laurence P. Feldman, which you will find at the back of this book. This should take about 60 of the 90 minutes suggested for this activity. As you read make notes and reflect on the following questions:

1 Do you think the concerns raised by Feldman are still valid today, more than three decades later?

2 Do you think many businesses today have proactively changed their marketing practices to emphasise non-material consumption and stress social criteria, as Feldman suggests they should?

3 Look back at your notes on Activity 2.1 earlier in this book. In this we introduced a business scenario where you are about to open a new café near where you live. Are there any societal or environmental issues that you should consider in this business?

Feedback

1 Although over thirty years have elapsed since Feldman wrote his article, many of the concerns remain pertinent today. Consumer choice and material consumption have increased rather than decreased since that time. What was then primarily true for North America and, to some extent, Western Europe, is now increasingly true for many so-called emerging economies, such as China. To some extent, the immediate concern at the time, with running out of environmental resources and raw materials, has diminished somewhat in the intervening years as new oil and other resources have been discovered. However, today we are concerned not so much with the availability of energy and other resources, but with the negative effects of their waste products, such as carbon dioxide, and related environmental issues (for example, global warming). The problems of balancing individual choice with societal well-being are still as critical as they were then.

2 Sadly, it would seem that business as a whole has made little progress in solving this dilemma. Marketing practice in general usually still seems to emphasise individual choice and material consumption over societal benefits and non-material consumption. It is true, however, that a growing number of businesses compete over the environmentally and societally benign nature of their products (see, for instance, the growth in fair trade products or environmental marketing, discussed below).

3 Even small businesses are affected by social concerns. The food industry, in particular, has frequently been criticised as many heavily advertised food products are thought to lead to obesity or other health problems. This criticism is directed mainly at large food processing businesses, but the questions involved have implications for small businesses, such as your café, as well. Whether or not your business may raise social concerns will depend on, among other things, the kind of food you serve and how you promote and price it. Will you be offering mostly fried foods or healthy options? Will you make any attempt to inform your customers about healthy foods and will you promote the healthy options in a particular way? Will healthy options be more expensive than the traditional fried food often served in cafés?

The basic principle that businesses should not only consider the immediate expectations of their customers, but should also take into account the long-term welfare of customers and society at large, is difficult to argue with. In essence, it still defines a business's social responsibility from a marketing perspective. But the societal marketing concept has also come under some criticism itself. Most of the critics say that the main problem is that it has not really made much difference in practice. For instance, Abratt and Sacks (1989) discovered that managers in large tobacco and alcohol processing businesses had never heard of the societal marketing concept. The same managers were not really prepared to accept that their businesses had a responsibility for the welfare of their customers and society. More recently, Crane and Desmond (2002) argued that the societal marketing concept was not a good basis on which one might make marketing practice and theory more socially responsible. The reasons for this, they argued, were that (a) there was not enough explicit moral responsibility in the societal marketing concept; (b) it was difficult to establish who should define what the interests of the consumer and of wider society were; and (c) there was too much emphasis on 'good' or 'bad' products, with not enough consideration of how and by whom these products were being used. Moreover, these authors argued, three decades after the development of the societal marketing concept social concerns over marketing had not only not gone away but had actually increased. This suggested that the societal marketing concept had not actually done the job it was expected to do.

'Isn't that the tobacco slogan we used in the sixties?'

The societal marketing concept is an overall theoretical framework that is intended to make marketers think about the social responsibility of marketing. There are also a number of *practices* by which businesses can try to make their marketing more socially responsible. Two of the better known of these practices are cause-related marketing and advocacy marketing (Drumwright and Murphy, 2001). We will look at these briefly below.

Cause-related marketing campaigns link contribution to charity to product sales. Here consumers make a purchase then, as a result, the company makes a donation to the cause. For example, an individual buys a particular brand of coffee and a small percentage of the amount paid goes to a fund that will help save the rainforests of the world. In advocacy advertising a business promotes a social cause, such as responsible drinking or healthy eating, through its own marketing communications. For instance, an advocacy advertisement message might focus on the dangers of extinction of certain wildlife species and try to persuade consumers to support the World Wildlife Fund's (WWF) efforts to save endangered species. Such marketing practices often provide much needed funds for good causes or can promote a social message with more money than government-sponsored advertising. However, the problems are that cause-related marketing often donates only a very small proportion of the sales revenue to good causes and advocacy advertising is often mistrusted by people, as they don't understand why a business should promote social causes.

So far, we have mainly considered social and environmental issues together. Many people, however, believe that environmental issues are too big to be considered as merely a subset of social problems. Environmental or 'green' marketing has become a topic in its own right and this is discussed in the next section.

5.2 'Green' marketing

As already mentioned above and in study Session 2, business activity in general, and marketing in particular, are influenced by, and have an impact on, the natural environment at every stage in the production and consumption process. This is from the sourcing of raw materials, through the production of goods and services and storing and transportation of finished goods, to the use of the product by the final consumer and its eventual disposal. As a result, there are a large number of well-known environmental problems which are largely or partly the result of human economic activity. Throop et al. (1993) list the following problems at local, regional and global level:

- *Inadequate solid waste disposal capacity* Modern society produces ever larger quantities of industrial and household waste, whereas suitable places for landfill sites and other forms of waste disposal become ever scarcer.

- *Air pollution* Industrial processes and consumer use of more and more machinery, including cars, leads to air pollution.

- *Declining fish and crustacean populations* Modern fishing fleets use high-tech methods to find and catch more and more fish, to a point where major fisheries worldwide have collapsed and are no longer commercially viable.

- *Topsoil erosion* This is a common problem associated with modern agriculture, particularly large-scale, industrial-style agriculture – heavy machinery disturbs top soils which are then blown away by wind or washed away by rain; logging of forests and increasing population pressure in ecologically sensitive areas also often leads to this problem.

- *Ozone depletion* CFCs (chlorofluorocarbon), a chemical once common in aerosols and refrigerators, is the main culprit of ozone depletion; the phasing out of such chemicals from consumer products and industrial processes may be able to reverse this process.

- *Marine and fresh water pollution* This results from industry, agriculture, households, shipping and other sources.

- *Toxic waste accumulation* Many toxic wastes, such as many artificial chemicals, accumulate in nature and can still be found – for instance, in marine mammals – years after their production and use has ceased.

- *Species extinction and reduction of biodiversity* Population pressure, intensive agriculture and industrial development all encroach on the habitats of plant and animal species and can lead to their extinction.

- *Wetlands destruction* This is one example of valuable wildlife habitats being destroyed by development; for instance, for housing, agriculture or industry.

- *Climate modification* Accelerated use of fossil fuels in industrial processes and consumption is thought to contribute to global climate change with unpredictable but potentially very serious consequences.

Many of these problems are not directly or exclusively related to marketing but to modern industrial societies in general. However, marketing plays an important part in the development of them. Conventional marketing practice has been criticised for its lack of ecological **sustainability**. In the context of the rise of consumer society, marketing practice has been criticised for promoting excessive consumption and materialism and thus the over-exploitation of natural resources for the production and use of consumer products. Another key criticism is that product design is often environmentally wasteful as many consumer products have only short durability, use excessive amounts of raw materials and are not being designed for recycling. No part of the marketing chain is without criticism. Excessive packaging, production of marketing materials and the transportation of finished goods, often over long distances, are all criticised as being wasteful (Velasquez, 2002).

'Green' marketing has been proposed as a solution, at least a partial one, to the environmental issues connected with conventional marketing. The logic behind it is that there is a rising consumer awareness of and concern about environmental issues. Consumers demand more environmentally responsible products and production processes. Marketers react flexibly to these consumer demands, changing products and processes to achieve the same consumer benefits with less environmental detriment. Those who do not respond are perceived by consumers to be environmentally irresponsible and are eventually pushed out of a competitive market.

Peattie and Charter (1994) identify a number of driving forces which encourage marketers to aim for more sustainable marketing practices, including:

- public opinion and changing societal values;
- green consumer demand and the opportunities of a growing market for environmentally friendly goods and technologies;
- internal and competitive pressures;
- legislation;
- green investment funds;
- interest from media and pressure groups;
- the cost to business from environmental disasters.

They argue that, in order to 'go green' successfully, marketers need to adopt a holistic view of the green marketing process, which includes an appreciation of and influence over all aspects of a business, its products and production system. Green marketing requires new types of information regarding the environmental performance of products, supplies, production processes and competitors. It also requires marketers to think in timescales of years or even decades, rather than months.

Many businesses have responded to these drivers for more environmentally friendly business and marketing practice. Environmentally concerned consumers can now buy a whole range of less environmentally harmful product alternatives, ranging from organic foodstuffs, more readily biodegradable detergents, low-energy light bulbs, more fuel-efficient cars, to paper products made from recycled paper, timber products from sustainable forestry, and many more.

The following activity is intended to help you reflect on some of the issues of green marketing.

Activity 5.2

Spend about **1 hour** on this activity

Purpose: to study the environmental issues surrounding wood-based consumer products.

Task: go to the website of the environmental pressure group Greenpeace (http://www.greenpeace.org.uk, or find it using an internet search engine, such as Google or Yahoo!) and click on the page 'What we do'. Select the page on 'Forests' and read what Greenpeace have to say about the threats to forest lands. Then put 'forest-friendly tissue and toilet roll' in the search field on the left hand side and click on the article 'Are your tissues wiping away the last remaining forests?'. Read through all these sections, including the information on the Forest Stewardship Council and make some notes. Alternatively, you could search for 'green' or 'forest-friendly' paper products online, using an internet search engine.

Now answer the following questions:

1 What does it mean in environmental terms if a product is Forest Stewardship Council (FSC) certified?

2 When you normally shop for paper products, do you ever look for information that tells you whether the products you buy are certified by the FSC? Why (not)?

3 Do you agree that consumers should take environmental responsibility and buy products that are environmentally friendly? Why, or why not?

4 Now think of the brand of tissue or toilet roll that you normally buy and check on the Greenpeace website how well it does in terms of forest friendliness.

Feedback

1 As stated in the information on the Greenpeace website, the Forest Stewardship Council is an international, non-government organisation which promotes responsible forest management. They have developed a system of forest certification and product labelling that allows timber merchants and consumers to identify wood from well-managed forests. Through this measure, the FCS is trying to encourage environmentally responsible customer behaviour.

2 There are several environmental labelling schemes for consumer products available, and retailers sometimes offer additional environmental information on their products. Many consumers look at some of this information but few manage to look at and act on all of it. You might have found yourself in a similar situation. A reason for not always taking in environmental information about products is that it is time consuming to attend to all this information; often too, it is not that easy to work out what really is the most environmentally responsible purchasing option, as there is so much information and it can be conflicting. Or you might have felt that other considerations, such as product quality or price, were more important to you.

3 Reasons for agreeing that consumers should buy environmentally friendly products are that this helps to preserve old-growth forests, particularly

tropical rainforests, which are vitally important for world climate and therefore have an impact on all human life. Reasons for disagreeing are that it may be inconvenient to try to find environmentally responsible products, that they may cost more and that individual consumers have little influence if others continue to behave in an environmentally detrimental way.

4　You may have found that the brand you normally use is quite forest friendly, and you probably feel satisfied with that. If you found that your favourite brand is not particularly forest friendly, perhaps this knowledge makes you think about switching brands, or perhaps you are thinking of other good reasons why you will still continue buying this brand.

While green marketing seems to have made some progress towards offering consumers more environmentally responsible product alternatives, the notion of 'green' marketing and 'green' consumption as a solution to environmental problems has also been criticised. If over-consumption is at the heart of many environmental problems, it may be difficult to see how more consumption, even of less environmentally harmful products, can be the solution. Kilbourne et al. (1997) argue that green marketing and consumption should be studied within a more general framework of the wider economic and social system which sustains a belief in the promise of abundance and ever greater levels of material accumulation.

According to Sagoff (1986, p. 229) individuals act differently as consumers than they do as citizens, namely that 'we act as consumers to get what we want for ourselves. We act as citizens to achieve what we think is right or best for the community'. The danger of approaching environmental problems as marketing problems is the reliance on individual consumer preferences which may reflect short-term 'selfish' desires and wants rather than a long-term appreciation of the common good. If consumers are not willing to pay for social and environmental 'goods' through their individual purchase behaviour, then such goods will not be supplied. In Sagoff's view the 'public' and 'shared' nature of environmental problems makes them more appropriate for public policy than for market solutions. This echoes some of the views expressed in Essential Reading 4.

It may be the case that concentrating on green consumer pressure and marketing often merely serves the purpose of patching over fundamental rifts between current Western lifestyles and the requirements of ecological balance, thus suggesting easy solutions where there may be none (Smith, 1998; Iyer, 1999). Welford (1997) even argues that all the talk about greener management and marketing only serves to mask business-as-usual behind the scenes and that business has 'hijacked' environmentalism for its own ends. You may have your own views on this argument; take a look at the appropriate section of the Study Companion to help guide your thinking.

5.3 Conclusion

In this study session we have discussed how businesses have tried to address the social and environmental concerns that are often associated with marketing. We looked at the societal marketing concept and its impact on marketing practice, as well as cause-related marketing and advocacy advertising. We then took a closer look at some of the environmental problems associated with business activity and how green marketing tries to address these. We hope that this study session and the book as a whole will have helped you form some of your own opinions about the positive and negative aspects of modern marketing practice.

5.4 Learning outcomes

By the end of this study session on addressing societal and environmental concerns in marketing you should be able to:

- define the societal marketing concept;
- discuss how the societal marketing concept and social marketing practice try to address common social and ethical concerns with marketing;
- explain what is meant by 'green' marketing;
- discuss the extent to which green marketing practice addresses environmental concerns with marketing.

You will have developed your learning by:

- reading the article by Laurence P. Feldman (Essential Reading 4) and discussing how his ideas apply today and to a particular business scenario;
- carrying out a web-based activity looking at DIY retailers' policies on green consumption and marketing.

Conclusion to Book 4

In this book we have studied marketing both from a 'micro-perspective', relating to the level of the business, and from a 'macro-perspective', relating to the level of stakeholders, the wider society and the natural environment.

The micro-perspective covered the meaning of a marketing orientation, market segmentation and the marketing mix. From a marketing orientation, which argues that businesses can only be consistently successful if they match their product offerings to customers' needs and expectations, follows the necessity to gain a good understanding of marketing environments and buyer behaviour, which was covered in study Sessions 2 and 3. Once marketers have that understanding, they can design a marketing mix that will appeal to buyers. Study Session 4 dealt with the marketing mix, including services marketing.

Throughout the book, we saw how marketing is not only a function to enhance business performance but has a wider role in society. One of the prime purposes of the marketing function is to deal with stakeholders outside the business. Marketers therefore have a particular duty to understand the needs of these stakeholders and to treat them in an ethically responsible way. These were discussed throughout the book and specifically in study Session 5, which looked at the societal marketing concept and green marketing.

Throughout the book, activities have been designed to help you make connections between the concepts covered and actual marketing practice, often as you might experience it as a consumer. Further commentary and reflection on these learning activities is available in the accompanying Study Companion.

After studying this book you should have gained a comprehensive overview of marketing as a social phenomenon, as well as a business function.

References

Abratt, R. and Sacks, D. (1989) 'Perceptions of the societal marketing concept', *European Journal of Marketing*, Vol. 23, No. 6, pp. 25–33.

American Marketing Association (2004) *Dictionary of Marketing Terms* [online], http://www.marketingpower.com (accessed 18 April 2006).

Assael, H. (1987) *Consumer Behaviour and Marketing Action*, Boston, MA, Kent Publishing.

Baudrillard, J. (1997) *The Consumer Society*, London, Sage.

Belk, R. W. (1995) 'Studies in the new consumer behaviour' in Miller, D. (ed.) *Acknowledging Consumption: A Review of New Studies*, London, Routledge, pp. 58–95.

Blythe, J. (2001) *Essentials of Marketing* (2nd edn), Harlow, Financial Times/Prentice Hall, Pearson Education Limited.

Bourdieu, P. (1984) Distinction: *A Social Critique of the Judgment of Taste*, London, Routledge.

Brassington, F. and Pettitt, S. (2005) *Essentials of Marketing*, Harlow, Financial Times/Prentice Hall.

Buttle, F. (1996) 'Relationship marketing' in Buttle, F. (ed.) *Relationship Marketing: Theory and Practice*, London, Paul Chapman Publishing, pp. 1–16.

Campbell, C. (1987) *The Romantic Ethic and the Spirit of Modern Consumerism*, Oxford, Macmillan.

Collins, J. C. and Porras, J. I. (1995) *Built to Last: Successful Habits of Visionary Companies*, New York, Harper Business, pp. 156–8.

Crane, A. and Desmond, J. (2002) 'Societal marketing and morality', *European Journal of Marketing*, Vol. 36, No. 5/6, pp. 548–69.

Crane, A. and Matten, D. (2004) *Business Ethics,* Oxford, Oxford University Press.

Crawford, C. M. (1991) *New Products Management*, Homewood, IL, Irwin.

Diamond, J. (2005) *Collapse: How Societies Choose to Fail or Survive*, London, Penguin/Allen Lane.

Douglas, M. and Isherwood, B. (1978) *The World of Goods: Towards an Anthropology of Consumption*, London, Allen Lane.

Drumwright, M. E. and Murphy, D. E. (2001) 'Corporate societal marketing' in Bloom, P. N. and Grundlack, G. T. (eds) *Handbook of Marketing and Society*, Thousand Oaks, CA, Sage, pp. 162–83.

Featherstone, M. (1991) *Consumer Culture and Postmodernism,* London, Sage.

Freeman, R. E. (1984) *Strategic Management: A Stakeholder Approach,* Boston, MA, Pitman.

Gabriel, Y. and Lang, T. (1995) *The Unmanageable Consumer: Contemporary Consumption and its Fragmentations*, London, Sage.

Giddens, A. (1991) *Modernity and Self-Identity*, Cambridge, Polity.

Grönroos, C. (1990) *Service Management and Marketing: Managing the Moments of Truth in Service Competition*, Lexington, MA, Free Press/ Lexington Books.

Guardian (2006) 'Endowment firm fined £750,000', Hilary Osborne and agencies in *The Guardian*, Business, 12 January.

Iyer, G. R. (1999) 'Business, consumers and sustainable living in an interconnected world: a multilateral ecocentric approach', *Journal of Business Ethics,* Vol. 20, pp. 273–88.

Kilbourne, W. (1998) 'Green marketing: a theoretical perspective', *Journal of Marketing Management*, Vol. 14, pp. 641–55.

Kilbourne, W., McDonagh, P. and Prothero, A. (1997) 'Sustainable consumption and the quality of life: a macro marketing challenge to the dominant social paradigm', *Journal of Macro Marketing,* Vol. 17, No. 1, pp. 4–24.

Kotler, P. (1972) 'What consumerism means for markets', *Harvard Business Review,* May–June, pp. 48–57.

Kotler, P., Armstrong, G., Saunders, F. and Wong, V. (2001) *Principles of Marketing*, 3rd European edn, Harlow, Financial Times/Prentice Hall, Pearson Education Limited.

McCracken, G. (1990) *Culture and Consumption*, Bloomington, IN, Indiana University Press.

Miles, S. (1998) *Consumerism: As a Way of Life*, London, Sage.

Mitsch, R. A. (1990) 'Three roads to innovation', *The Journal of Business Strategy*, September/October, pp. 18–21.

Peattie, K. and Charter, M. (1994) 'Green marketing' in Baker, M. J. (ed.) *The Marketing Book*, 3rd edn, Oxford and Boston, MA, Butterworth-Heinemann, pp. 691–712.

Porter, M. E. (1990) 'How competitive forces shape strategy', *Harvard Business Review*, Vol. 57, No. 2, March–April, pp. 137–45.

Reitz, H. J., Wall, J. A. Jr and Love, M. S. (1998) 'Ethics in negotiation: oil and water or good lubrication', *Business Horizons*, May–June, pp. 5–14.

Sagoff, M. (1986) 'At the shrine of Our Lady of Fatima, or why political questions are not all economic' in VanDeVeer, D. and Pierce, C. (eds) *People, Penguins and Plastic Trees: Basic Issues in Environmental Ethics,* Belmont, CA, Wadsworth.

Smith, N. C. and Cooper-Martin, E. (1997) 'Ethics and target marketing: the role of product harm and consumer vulnerability', *Journal of Marketing,* Vol. 61, July, pp. 1–20.

Smith, N. C. and Quelch, J. A. (1993) *Ethics in Marketing,* Homewood, IL, Irwin.

Smith, T. (1998) *The Green Marketing Myth: Tending our Goats at the Edge of Apocalypse*, Toronto, University of Toronto Press.

Throop, G. M., Starik, M. and Rands, G. (1993) 'Sustainable strategy in a greening world', *Advances in Strategic Management*, Vol. 9, pp. 63–92.

Veblen, T. (1925 [1899]) *The Theory of the Leisure Class: An Economic Study of Institutions*, London, George Allen and Unwin.

Velasquez, M. (2002) *Business Ethics: Concepts and Cases*, Upper Saddle River, NJ, Prentice Hall.

Welford, R. (1997) *Hijacking Environmentalism: Corporate Responses to Sustainable Development*, London, Earthscan.

Essential Reading 1

'Marketing myopia' by Theodore Levitt is on the next page

(Source: Levitt, T., 1960, 'Marketing myopia', *Harvard Business Review*, Vol. 34, No.4, July–August, pp. 45–56.)

*Sustained growth depends on how broadly you define your business—
and how carefully you gauge your customers' needs.*

BEST OF HBR 1960

Marketing Myopia

by Theodore Levitt

We always know when an HBR article hits the big time. Journalists write about it, pundits talk about it, executives route copies of it around the organization, and its vocabulary becomes familiar to managers everywhere—sometimes to the point where they don't even associate the words with the original article. Most important, of course, managers change how they do business because the ideas in the piece helped them see issues in a new light.

"Marketing Myopia" is the quintessential big hit HBR piece. In it, Theodore Levitt, who was then a lecturer in business administration at the Harvard Business School, introduced the famous question, "What business are you really in?" and with it the claim that, had railroad executives seen themselves as being in the transportation business rather than the railroad business, they would have continued to grow. The article is as much about strategy as it is about marketing, but it also introduced the most influential marketing idea of the past half-century: that businesses will do better in the end if they concentrate on meeting customers' needs rather than on selling prod-

ucts. "Marketing Myopia" won the McKinsey Award in 1960.

Every major industry was once a growth industry. But some that are now riding a wave of growth enthusiasm are very much in the shadow of decline. Others that are thought of as seasoned growth industries have actually stopped growing. In every case, the reason growth is threatened, slowed, or stopped is *not* because the market is saturated. It is because there has been a failure of management.

Fateful Purposes

The failure is at the top. The executives responsible for it, in the last analysis, are those who deal with broad aims and policies. Thus:

• The railroads did not stop growing because the need for passenger and freight transportation declined. That grew. The railroads are in trouble today not because that need was filled by others (cars, trucks, airplanes, and even telephones) but because it was *not* filled by the railroads themselves. They let others take customers away from them because they assumed themselves to be in the railroad business rather than in the transportation business. The reason they defined their industry incorrectly was that they were railroad oriented instead of transportation oriented; they were product oriented instead of customer oriented.

• Hollywood barely escaped being totally ravished by television. Actually, all the established film companies went through drastic reorganizations. Some simply disappeared. All of them got into trouble not because of TV's inroads but because of their own myopia. As with the railroads, Hollywood defined its business incorrectly. It thought it was in the movie business when it was actually in the entertainment business. "Movies" implied a specific, limited product. This produced a fatuous contentment that from the beginning led producers to view TV as a threat. Hollywood scorned and rejected TV when it should have welcomed it as an opportunity—an opportunity to expand the entertainment business.

Today, TV is a bigger business than the old narrowly defined movie business ever was. Had Hollywood been customer oriented (providing entertainment) rather than product oriented (making movies), would it have gone through the fiscal purgatory that it did? I doubt it. What ultimately saved Hollywood and accounted for its resurgence was the wave of new young writers, producers, and directors whose previous successes in television had decimated the old movie companies and toppled the big movie moguls.

There are other, less obvious examples of industries that have been and are now endangering their futures by improperly defining their purposes. I shall discuss some of them in detail later and analyze the kind of policies that lead to trouble. Right now, it may help to show what a thoroughly customer-oriented management can do to keep a growth industry growing, even after the obvious opportunities have been exhausted, and here there are two examples that have been around for a long time. They are nylon and glass—specifically, E.I. du Pont de Nemours and Company and Corning Glass Works.

Both companies have great technical competence. Their product orientation is unquestioned. But this alone does not explain their success. After all, who was more pridefully product oriented and product conscious than

the erstwhile New England textile companies that have been so thoroughly massacred? The DuPonts and the Cornings have succeeded not primarily because of their product or research orientation but because they have been thoroughly customer oriented also. It is constant watchfulness for opportunities to apply their technical know-how to the creation of customer-satisfying uses that accounts for their prodigious output of successful new products. Without a very sophisticated eye on the customer, most of their new products might have been wrong, their sales methods useless.

Aluminum has also continued to be a growth industry, thanks to the efforts of two wartime-created companies that deliberately set about inventing new customer-satisfying uses. Without Kaiser Aluminum & Chemical Corporation and Reynolds Metals Company, the total demand for aluminum today would be vastly less.

Error of Analysis. Some may argue that it is foolish to set the railroads off against aluminum or the movies off against glass. Are not aluminum and glass naturally so versatile that the industries are bound to have more growth opportunities than the railroads and the movies? This view commits precisely the error I have been talking about. It defines an industry or a product or a cluster of know-how so narrowly as to guarantee its premature senescence. When we mention "railroads," we should make sure we mean "transportation." As transporters, the railroads still have a good chance for very considerable growth. They are not limited to the railroad business as such (though in my opinion, rail transportation is potentially a much stronger transportation medium than is generally believed).

What the railroads lack is not opportunity but some of the managerial imaginativeness and audacity that made them great. Even an amateur like Jacques Barzun can see what is lacking when he says, "I grieve to see the most advanced physical and social organization of the last century go down in shabby disgrace for lack of the same comprehensive imagination that built it up. [What is lacking is] the will of the companies to survive and to satisfy the public by inventiveness and skill."[1]

Shadow of Obsolescence

It is impossible to mention a single major industry that did not at one time qualify for the

Theodore Levitt, a longtime professor of marketing at Harvard Business School in Boston, is now professor emeritus. His most recent books are *Thinking About Management* (1990) and *The Marketing Imagination* (1983), both from Free Press.

magic appellation of "growth industry." In each case, the industry's assumed strength lay in the apparently unchallenged superiority of its product. There appeared to be no effective substitute for it. It was itself a runaway substitute for the product it so triumphantly replaced. Yet one after another of these celebrated industries has come under a shadow. Let us look briefly at a few more of them, this time taking examples that have so far received a little less attention.

Dry Cleaning. This was once a growth industry with lavish prospects. In an age of wool garments, imagine being finally able to get them clean safely and easily. The boom was on. Yet here we are 30 years after the boom started, and the industry is in trouble. Where has the competition come from? From a better way of cleaning? No. It has come from synthetic fibers and chemical additives that have cut the need for dry cleaning. But this is only the beginning. Lurking in the wings and ready to make chemical dry cleaning totally obsolete is that powerful magician, ultrasonics.

Electric Utilities. This is another one of those supposedly "no substitute" products that has been enthroned on a pedestal of invincible growth. When the incandescent lamp came along, kerosene lights were finished. Later, the waterwheel and the steam engine were cut to ribbons by the flexibility, reliability, simplicity, and just plain easy availability of electric motors. The prosperity of electric utilities continues to wax extravagant as the home is converted into a museum of electric gadgetry. How can anybody miss by investing in utilities, with no competition, nothing but growth ahead?

But a second look is not quite so comforting. A score of nonutility companies are well advanced toward developing a powerful chemical fuel cell, which could sit in some hidden closet of every home silently ticking off electric power. The electric lines that vulgarize so many neighborhoods would be eliminated. So would the endless demolition of streets and service interruptions during storms. Also on the horizon is solar energy, again pioneered by nonutility companies.

Who says that the utilities have no competition? They may be natural monopolies now, but tomorrow they may be natural deaths. To avoid this prospect, they too will have to develop fuel cells, solar energy, and other power sources. To survive, they themselves will have to plot the obsolescence of what now produces their livelihood.

Grocery Stores. Many people find it hard to realize that there ever was a thriving establishment known as the "corner store." The supermarket took over with a powerful effectiveness. Yet the big food chains of the 1930s narrowly escaped being completely wiped out by the aggressive expansion of independent supermarkets. The first genuine supermarket was opened in 1930, in Jamaica, Long Island. By 1933, supermarkets were thriving in California, Ohio, Pennsylvania, and elsewhere. Yet the established chains pompously ignored them. When they chose to notice them, it was with such derisive descriptions as "cheapy," "horse-and-buggy," "cracker-barrel storekeeping," and "unethical opportunists."

The executive of one big chain announced at the time that he found it "hard to believe that people will drive for miles to shop for foods and sacrifice the personal service chains have perfected and to which [the consumer] is accustomed."[2] As late as 1936, the National Wholesale Grocers convention and the New Jersey Retail Grocers Association said there was nothing to fear. They said that the supers' narrow appeal to the price buyer limited the size of their market. They had to draw from miles around. When imitators came, there would be wholesale liquidations as volume fell. The high sales of the supers were said to be partly due to their novelty. People wanted convenient neighborhood grocers. If the neighborhood stores would "cooperate with their suppliers, pay attention to their costs, and improve their service," they would be able to weather the competition until it blew over.[3]

It never blew over. The chains discovered that survival required going into the supermarket business. This meant the wholesale destruction of their huge investments in corner store sites and in established distribution and merchandising methods. The companies with "the courage of their convictions" resolutely stuck to the corner store philosophy. They kept their pride but lost their shirts.

A Self-Deceiving Cycle. But memories are short. For example, it is hard for people who today confidently hail the twin messiahs of electronics and chemicals to see how things could possibly go wrong with these galloping industries. They probably also cannot see how

It is hard for people who hail the twin messiahs of electronics and chemicals to see how things could possibly go wrong with these galloping industries.

a reasonably sensible businessperson could have been as myopic as the famous Boston millionaire who early in the twentieth century unintentionally sentenced his heirs to poverty by stipulating that his entire estate be forever invested exclusively in electric streetcar securities. His posthumous declaration, "There will always be a big demand for efficient urban transportation," is no consolation to his heirs, who sustain life by pumping gasoline at automobile filling stations.

Yet, in a casual survey I took among a group of intelligent business executives, nearly half agreed that it would be hard to hurt their heirs by tying their estates forever to the electronics industry. When I then confronted them with the Boston streetcar example, they chorused unanimously, "That's different!" But is it? Is not the basic situation identical?

In truth, *there is no such thing as a growth industry*, I believe. There are only companies organized and operated to create and capitalize on growth opportunities. Industries that assume themselves to be riding some automatic growth escalator invariably descend into stagnation. The history of every dead and dying "growth" industry shows a self-deceiving cycle of bountiful expansion and undetected decay. There are four conditions that usually guarantee this cycle:

1. The belief that growth is assured by an expanding and more affluent population;

2. The belief that there is no competitive substitute for the industry's major product;

3. Too much faith in mass production and in the advantages of rapidly declining unit costs as output rises;

4. Preoccupation with a product that lends itself to carefully controlled scientific experimentation, improvement, and manufacturing cost reduction.

I should like now to examine each of these conditions in some detail. To build my case as boldly as possible, I shall illustrate the points with reference to three industries: petroleum, automobiles, and electronics. I'll focus on petroleum in particular, because it spans more years and more vicissitudes. Not only do these three industries have excellent reputations with the general public and also enjoy the confidence of sophisticated investors, but their managements have become known for progressive thinking in areas like financial control, product research, and management training. If

obsolescence can cripple even these industries, it can happen anywhere.

Population Myth

The belief that profits are assured by an expanding and more affluent population is dear to the heart of every industry. It takes the edge off the apprehensions everybody understandably feels about the future. If consumers are multiplying and also buying more of your product or service, you can face the future with considerably more comfort than if the market were shrinking. An expanding market keeps the manufacturer from having to think very hard or imaginatively. If thinking is an intellectual response to a problem, then the absence of a problem leads to the absence of thinking. If your product has an automatically expanding market, then you will not give much thought to how to expand it.

One of the most interesting examples of this is provided by the petroleum industry. Probably our oldest growth industry, it has an enviable record. While there are some current concerns about its growth rate, the industry itself tends to be optimistic.

But I believe it can be demonstrated that it is undergoing a fundamental yet typical change. It is not only ceasing to be a growth industry but may actually be a declining one, relative to other businesses. Although there is widespread unawareness of this fact, it is conceivable that in time, the oil industry may find itself in much the same position of retrospective glory that the railroads are now in. Despite its pioneering work in developing and applying the present-value method of investment evaluation, in employee relations, and in working with developing countries, the petroleum business is a distressing example of how complacency and wrongheadedness can stubbornly convert opportunity into near disaster.

One of the characteristics of this and other industries that have believed very strongly in the beneficial consequences of an expanding population, while at the same time having a generic product for which there has appeared to be no competitive substitute, is that the individual companies have sought to outdo their competitors by improving on what they are already doing. This makes sense, of course, if one assumes that sales are tied to the country's population strings, because the customer can compare products only on a feature-by-feature basis. I believe it is significant, for example, that not since John D. Rockefeller sent free kerosene lamps to China has the oil industry done anything really outstanding to create a demand for its product. Not even in product improvement has it showered itself with eminence. The greatest single improvement—the development of tetraethyl lead—came from outside the industry, specifically from General Motors and DuPont. The big contributions made by the industry itself are confined to the technology of oil exploration, oil production, and oil refining.

Asking for Trouble. In other words, the petroleum industry's efforts have focused on improving the *efficiency* of getting and making its product, not really on improving the generic product or its marketing. Moreover, its chief product has continually been defined in the narrowest possible terms—namely, gasoline, not energy, fuel, or transportation. This attitude has helped assure that:

• Major improvements in gasoline quality tend not to originate in the oil industry. The development of superior alternative fuels also comes from outside the oil industry, as will be shown later.

• Major innovations in automobile fuel marketing come from small, new oil companies that are not primarily preoccupied with production or refining. These are the companies that have been responsible for the rapidly expanding multipump gasoline stations, with their successful emphasis on large and clean layouts, rapid and efficient driveway service, and quality gasoline at low prices.

Thus, the oil industry is asking for trouble from outsiders. Sooner or later, in this land of hungry investors and entrepreneurs, a threat is sure to come. The possibility of this will become more apparent when we turn to the next dangerous belief of many managements. For the sake of continuity, because this second belief is tied closely to the first, I shall continue with the same example.

The Idea of Indispensability. The petroleum industry is pretty much convinced that there is no competitive substitute for its major product, gasoline—or, if there is, that it will continue to be a derivative of crude oil, such as diesel fuel or kerosene jet fuel.

There is a lot of automatic wishful thinking in this assumption. The trouble is that most refining companies own huge amounts of crude oil reserves. These have value only if there is a market for products into which oil can be converted. Hence the tenacious belief in the continuing competitive superiority of automobile fuels made from crude oil.

This idea persists despite all historic evidence against it. The evidence not only shows that oil has never been a superior product for any purpose for very long but also that the oil industry has never really been a growth industry. Rather, it has been a succession of different businesses that have gone through the usual historic cycles of growth, maturity, and decay. The industry's overall survival is owed to a series of miraculous escapes from total obsolescence, of last-minute and unexpected reprieves from total disaster reminiscent of the perils of Pauline.

The Perils of Petroleum. To illustrate, I shall sketch in only the main episodes. First, crude oil was largely a patent medicine. But even before that fad ran out, demand was greatly expanded by the use of oil in kerosene lamps. The prospect of lighting the world's lamps gave rise to an extravagant promise of growth. The prospects were similar to those the industry now holds for gasoline in other parts of the world. It can hardly wait for the underdeveloped nations to get a car in every garage.

In the days of the kerosene lamp, the oil companies competed with each other and against gaslight by trying to improve the illuminating characteristics of kerosene. Then suddenly the impossible happened. Edison invented a light that was totally nondependent on crude oil. Had it not been for the growing use of kerosene in space heaters, the incandescent lamp would have completely finished oil as a growth industry at that time. Oil would have been good for little else than axle grease.

Then disaster and reprieve struck again. Two great innovations occurred, neither originating in the oil industry. First, the successful development of coal-burning domestic central-heating systems made the space heater obsolete. While the industry reeled, along came its most magnificent boost yet: the internal combustion engine, also invented by outsiders. Then, when the prodigious expansion for gasoline finally began to level off in the 1920s, along came the miraculous escape of the central oil heater. Once again, the escape was pro-

The history of every dead and dying "growth" industry shows a self-deceiving cycle of bountiful expansion and undetected decay.

vided by an outsider's invention and development. And when that market weakened, wartime demand for aviation fuel came to the rescue. After the war, the expansion of civilian aviation, the dieselization of railroads, and the explosive demand for cars and trucks kept the industry's growth in high gear.

Meanwhile, centralized oil heating—whose boom potential had only recently been proclaimed—ran into severe competition from natural gas. While the oil companies themselves owned the gas that now competed with their oil, the industry did not originate the natural gas revolution, nor has it to this day greatly profited from its gas ownership. The gas revolution was made by newly formed transmission companies that marketed the product with an aggressive ardor. They started a magnificent new industry, first against the advice and then against the resistance of the oil companies.

By all the logic of the situation, the oil companies themselves should have made the gas revolution. They not only owned the gas, they also were the only people experienced in handling, scrubbing, and using it and the only people experienced in pipeline technology and transmission. They also understood heating problems. But, partly because they knew that natural gas would compete with their own sale of heating oil, the oil companies pooh-poohed the potential of gas. The revolution was finally started by oil pipeline executives who, unable to persuade their own companies to go into gas, quit and organized the spectacularly successful gas transmission companies. Even after their success became painfully evident to the oil companies, the latter did not go into gas transmission. The multibillion-dollar business that should have been theirs went to others. As in the past, the industry was blinded by its narrow preoccupation with a specific product and the value of its reserves. It paid little or no attention to its customers' basic needs and preferences.

The postwar years have not witnessed any change. Immediately after World War II, the oil industry was greatly encouraged about its future by the rapid increase in demand for its traditional line of products. In 1950, most companies projected annual rates of domestic expansion of around 6% through at least 1975. Though the ratio of crude oil reserves to demand in the free world was about 20 to 1, with 10 to 1 being usually considered a reasonable

> *If thinking is an intellectual response to a problem, then the absence of a problem leads to the absence of thinking.*

working ratio in the United States, booming demand sent oil explorers searching for more without sufficient regard to what the future really promised. In 1952, they "hit" in the Middle East; the ratio skyrocketed to 42 to 1. If gross additions to reserves continue at the average rate of the past five years (37 billion barrels annually), then by 1970, the reserve ratio will be up to 45 to 1. This abundance of oil has weakened crude and product prices all over the world.

An Uncertain Future. Management cannot find much consolation today in the rapidly expanding petrochemical industry, another oil-using idea that did not originate in the leading firms. The total U.S. production of petrochemicals is equivalent to about 2% (by volume) of the demand for all petroleum products. Although the petrochemical industry is now expected to grow by about 10% per year, this will not offset other drains on the growth of crude oil consumption. Furthermore, while petrochemical products are many and growing, it is important to remember that there are nonpetroleum sources of the basic raw material, such as coal. Besides, a lot of plastics can be produced with relatively little oil. A 50,000-barrel-per-day oil refinery is now considered the absolute minimum size for efficiency. But a 5,000-barrel-per-day chemical plant is a giant operation.

Oil has never been a continuously strong growth industry. It has grown by fits and starts, always miraculously saved by innovations and developments not of its own making. The reason it has not grown in a smooth progression is that each time it thought it had a superior product safe from the possibility of competitive substitutes, the product turned out to be inferior and notoriously subject to obsolescence. Until now, gasoline (for motor fuel, anyhow) has escaped this fate. But, as we shall see later, it too may be on its last legs.

The point of all this is that there is no guarantee against product obsolescence. If a company's own research does not make a product obsolete, another's will. Unless an industry is especially lucky, as oil has been until now, it can easily go down in a sea of red figures—just as the railroads have, as the buggy whip manufacturers have, as the corner grocery chains have, as most of the big movie companies have, and, indeed, as many other industries have.

The best way for a firm to be lucky is to make its own luck. That requires knowing what makes a business successful. One of the greatest enemies of this knowledge is mass production.

Production Pressures

Mass production industries are impelled by a great drive to produce all they can. The prospect of steeply declining unit costs as output rises is more than most companies can usually resist. The profit possibilities look spectacular. All effort focuses on production. The result is that marketing gets neglected.

John Kenneth Galbraith contends that just the opposite occurs.[4] Output is so prodigious that all effort concentrates on trying to get rid of it. He says this accounts for singing commercials, the desecration of the countryside with advertising signs, and other wasteful and vulgar practices. Galbraith has a finger on something real, but he misses the strategic point. Mass production does indeed generate great pressure to "move" the product. But what usually gets emphasized is selling, not marketing. Marketing, a more sophisticated and complex process, gets ignored.

The difference between marketing and selling is more than semantic. Selling focuses on the needs of the seller, marketing on the needs of the buyer. Selling is preoccupied with the seller's need to convert the product into cash, marketing with the idea of satisfying the needs of the customer by means of the product and the whole cluster of things associated with creating, delivering, and, finally, consuming it.

In some industries, the enticements of full mass production have been so powerful that top management in effect has told the sales department, "You get rid of it; we'll worry about profits." By contrast, a truly marketing-minded firm tries to create value-satisfying goods and services that consumers will want to buy. What it offers for sale includes not only the generic product or service but also how it is made available to the customer, in what form, when, under what conditions, and at what terms of trade. Most important, what it offers for sale is determined not by the seller but by the buyer. The seller takes cues from the buyer in such a way that the product becomes a consequence of the marketing effort, not vice versa.

A Lag in Detroit. This may sound like an elementary rule of business, but that does not keep it from being violated wholesale. It is certainly more violated than honored. Take the automobile industry.

Here mass production is most famous, most honored, and has the greatest impact on the entire society. The industry has hitched its fortune to the relentless requirements of the annual model change, a policy that makes customer orientation an especially urgent necessity. Consequently, the auto companies annually spend millions of dollars on consumer research. But the fact that the new compact cars are selling so well in their first year indicates that Detroit's vast researches have for a long time failed to reveal what customers really wanted. Detroit was not convinced that people wanted anything different from what they had been getting until it lost millions of customers to other small-car manufacturers.

How could this unbelievable lag behind consumer wants have been perpetuated for so long? Why did not research reveal consumer preferences before consumers' buying decisions themselves revealed the facts? Is that not what consumer research is for—to find out before the fact what is going to happen? The answer is that Detroit never really researched customers' wants. It only researched their preferences between the kinds of things it had already decided to offer them. For Detroit is mainly product oriented, not customer oriented. To the extent that the customer is recognized as having needs that the manufacturer should try to satisfy, Detroit usually acts as if the job can be done entirely by product changes. Occasionally, attention gets paid to financing, too, but that is done more in order to sell than to enable the customer to buy.

As for taking care of other customer needs, there is not enough being done to write about. The areas of the greatest unsatisfied needs are ignored or, at best, get stepchild attention. These are at the point of sale and on the matter of automotive repair and maintenance. Detroit views these problem areas as being of secondary importance. That is underscored by the fact that the retailing and servicing ends of this industry are neither owned and operated nor controlled by the manufacturers. Once the car is produced, things are pretty much in the dealer's inadequate hands. Illustrative of Detroit's arms-length attitude is the fact that, while servicing holds enormous sales-stimulating, profit-building opportunities, only 57 of Chevrolet's 7,000 dealers provide night maintenance service.

Motorists repeatedly express their dissatisfaction with servicing and their apprehensions about buying cars under the present selling setup. The anxieties and problems they encounter during the auto buying and maintenance processes are probably more intense and widespread today than many years ago. Yet the automobile companies do not seem to listen to or take their cues from the anguished consumer. If they do listen, it must be through the filter of their own preoccupation with production. The marketing effort is still viewed as a necessary consequence of the product—not vice versa, as it should be. That is the legacy of mass production, with its parochial view that profit resides essentially in low-cost full production.

What Ford Put First. The profit lure of mass production obviously has a place in the plans and strategy of business management, but it must always *follow* hard thinking about the customer. This is one of the most important lessons we can learn from the contradictory behavior of Henry Ford. In a sense, Ford was both the most brilliant and the most senseless marketer in American history. He was senseless because he refused to give the customer anything but a black car. He was brilliant because he fashioned a production system designed to fit market needs. We habitually celebrate him for the wrong reason: for his production genius. His real genius was marketing. We think he was able to cut his selling price and therefore sell millions of $500 cars because his invention of the assembly line had reduced the costs. Actually, he invented the assembly line because he had concluded that at $500 he could sell millions of cars. Mass production was the *result*, not the cause, of his low prices.

Ford emphasized this point repeatedly, but a nation of production-oriented business managers refuses to hear the great lesson he taught. Here is his operating philosophy as he expressed it succinctly:

> Our policy is to reduce the price, extend the operations, and improve the article. You will notice that the reduction of price comes first. We have never considered any costs as fixed. Therefore we first reduce the price to the point where we believe more sales will result. Then we go ahead and try to make the prices. We do

not bother about the costs. The new price forces the costs down. The more usual way is to take the costs and then determine the price; and although that method may be scientific in the narrow sense, it is not scientific in the broad sense, because what earthly use is it to know the cost if it tells you that you cannot manufacture at a price at which the article can be sold? But more to the point is the fact that, although one may calculate what a cost is, and of course all of our costs are carefully calculated, no one knows what a cost ought to be. One of the ways of discovering…is to name a price so low as to force everybody in the place to the highest point of efficiency. The low price makes everybody dig for profits. We make more discoveries concerning manufacturing and selling under this forced method than by any method of leisurely investigation.[5]

Product Provincialism. The tantalizing profit possibilities of low unit production costs may be the most seriously self-deceiving attitude that can afflict a company, particularly a "growth" company, where an apparently assured expansion of demand already tends to undermine a proper concern for the importance of marketing and the customer.

The usual result of this narrow preoccupation with so-called concrete matters is that instead of growing, the industry declines. It usually means that the product fails to adapt to the constantly changing patterns of consumer needs and tastes, to new and modified marketing institutions and practices, or to product developments in competing or complementary industries. The industry has its eyes so firmly on its own specific product that it does not see how it is being made obsolete.

The classic example of this is the buggy whip industry. No amount of product improvement could stave off its death sentence. But had the industry defined itself as being in the transportation business rather than in the buggy whip business, it might have survived. It would have done what survival always entails—that is, change. Even if it had only defined its business as providing a stimulant or catalyst to an energy source, it might have survived by becoming a manufacturer of, say, fan belts or air cleaners.

What may someday be a still more classic example is, again, the oil industry. Having let others steal marvelous opportunities from it (including natural gas, as already mentioned;

The marketing effort is still viewed as a necessary consequence of the product—not vice versa, as it should be.

missile fuels; and jet engine lubricants), one would expect it to have taken steps never to let that happen again. But this is not the case. We are now seeing extraordinary new developments in fuel systems specifically designed to power automobiles. Not only are these developments concentrated in firms outside the petroleum industry, but petroleum is almost systematically ignoring them, securely content in its wedded bliss to oil. It is the story of the kerosene lamp versus the incandescent lamp all over again. Oil is trying to improve hydrocarbon fuels rather than develop *any* fuels best suited to the needs of their users, whether or not made in different ways and with different raw materials from oil.

Here are some things that nonpetroleum companies are working on:

• More than a dozen such firms now have advanced working models of energy systems which, when perfected, will replace the internal combustion engine and eliminate the demand for gasoline. The superior merit of each of these systems is their elimination of frequent, time-consuming, and irritating refueling stops. Most of these systems are fuel cells designed to create electrical energy directly from chemicals without combustion. Most of them use chemicals that are not derived from oil—generally, hydrogen and oxygen.

• Several other companies have advanced models of electric storage batteries designed to power automobiles. One of these is an aircraft producer that is working jointly with several electric utility companies. The latter hope to use off-peak generating capacity to supply overnight plug-in battery regeneration. Another company, also using the battery approach, is a medium-sized electronics firm with extensive small-battery experience that it developed in connection with its work on hearing aids. It is collaborating with an automobile manufacturer. Recent improvements arising from the need for high-powered miniature power storage plants in rockets have put us within reach of a relatively small battery capable of withstanding great overloads or surges of power. Germanium diode applications and batteries using sintered plate and nickel cadmium techniques promise to make a revolution in our energy sources.

• Solar energy conversion systems are also getting increasing attention. One usually cautious Detroit auto executive recently ventured that solar-powered cars might be common by 1980.

As for the oil companies, they are more or less "watching developments," as one research director put it to me. A few are doing a bit of research on fuel cells, but this research is almost always confined to developing cells powered by hydrocarbon chemicals. None of them is enthusiastically researching fuel cells, batteries, or solar power plants. None of them is spending a fraction as much on research in these profoundly important areas as it is on the usual run-of-the-mill things like reducing combustion chamber deposits in gasoline engines. One major integrated petroleum company recently took a tentative look at the fuel cell and concluded that although "the companies actively working on it indicate a belief in ultimate success...the timing and magnitude of its impact are too remote to warrant recognition in our forecasts."

One might, of course, ask, Why should the oil companies do anything different? Would not chemical fuel cells, batteries, or solar energy kill the present product lines? The answer is that they would indeed, and that is precisely the reason for the oil firms' having to develop these power units before their competitors do, so they will not be companies without an industry.

Management might be more likely to do what is needed for its own preservation if it thought of itself as being in the energy business. But even that will not be enough if it persists in imprisoning itself in the narrow grip of its tight product orientation. It has to think of itself as taking care of customer needs, not finding, refining, or even selling oil. Once it genuinely thinks of its business as taking care of people's transportation needs, nothing can stop it from creating its own extravagantly profitable growth.

Creative Destruction. Since words are cheap and deeds are dear, it may be appropriate to indicate what this kind of thinking involves and leads to. Let us start at the beginning: the customer. It can be shown that motorists strongly dislike the bother, delay, and experience of buying gasoline. People actually do not buy gasoline. They cannot see it, taste it, feel it, appreciate it, or really test it. What they buy is the right to continue driving their cars. The gas station is like a tax collector to whom people are compelled to pay a peri-

It is not surprising that, having created a successful company by making a superior product, management continues to be oriented toward the product rather than the people who consume it.

odic toll as the price of using their cars. This makes the gas station a basically unpopular institution. It can never be made popular or pleasant, only less unpopular, less unpleasant.

Reducing its unpopularity completely means eliminating it. Nobody likes a tax collector, not even a pleasantly cheerful one. Nobody likes to interrupt a trip to buy a phantom product, not even from a handsome Adonis or a seductive Venus. Hence, companies that are working on exotic fuel substitutes that will eliminate the need for frequent refueling are heading directly into the outstretched arms of the irritated motorist. They are riding a wave of inevitability, not because they are creating something that is technologically superior or more sophisticated but because they are satisfying a powerful customer need. They are also eliminating noxious odors and air pollution.

Once the petroleum companies recognize the customer-satisfying logic of what another power system can do, they will see that they have no more choice about working on an efficient, long-lasting fuel (or some way of delivering present fuels without bothering the motorist) than the big food chains had a choice about going into the supermarket business or the vacuum tube companies had a choice about making semiconductors. For their own good, the oil firms will have to destroy their own highly profitable assets. No amount of wishful thinking can save them from the necessity of engaging in this form of "creative destruction."

I phrase the need as strongly as this because I think management must make quite an effort to break itself loose from conventional ways. It is all too easy in this day and age for a company or industry to let its sense of purpose become dominated by the economies of full production and to develop a dangerously lopsided product orientation. In short, if management lets itself drift, it invariably drifts in the direction of thinking of itself as producing goods and services, not customer satisfactions. While it probably will not descend to the depths of telling its salespeople, "You get rid of it; we'll worry about profits," it can, without knowing it, be practicing precisely that formula for withering decay. The historic fate of one growth industry after another has been its suicidal product provincialism.

Dangers of R&D

Another big danger to a firm's continued growth arises when top management is wholly transfixed by the profit possibilities of technical research and development. To illustrate, I shall turn first to a new industry—electronics—and then return once more to the oil companies. By comparing a fresh example with a familiar one, I hope to emphasize the prevalence and insidiousness of a hazardous way of thinking.

Marketing Shortchanged. In the case of electronics, the greatest danger that faces the glamorous new companies in this field is not that they do not pay enough attention to research and development but that they pay too much attention to it. And the fact that the fastest-growing electronics firms owe their eminence to their heavy emphasis on technical research is completely beside the point. They have vaulted to affluence on a sudden crest of unusually strong general receptiveness to new technical ideas. Also, their success has been shaped in the virtually guaranteed market of military subsidies and by military orders that in many cases actually preceded the existence of facilities to make the products. Their expansion has, in other words, been almost totally devoid of marketing effort.

Thus, they are growing up under conditions that come dangerously close to creating the illusion that a superior product will sell itself. It is not surprising that, having created a successful company by making a superior product, management continues to be oriented toward the product rather than the people who consume it. It develops the philosophy that continued growth is a matter of continued product innovation and improvement.

A number of other factors tend to strengthen and sustain this belief:

1. Because electronic products are highly complex and sophisticated, managements become top-heavy with engineers and scientists. This creates a selective bias in favor of research and production at the expense of marketing. The organization tends to view itself as making things rather than as satisfying customer needs. Marketing gets treated as a residual activity, "something else" that must be done once the vital job of product creation and production is completed.

2. To this bias in favor of product research, development, and production is added the bias

in favor of dealing with controllable variables. Engineers and scientists are at home in the world of concrete things like machines, test tubes, production lines, and even balance sheets. The abstractions to which they feel kindly are those that are testable or manipulatable in the laboratory or, if not testable, then functional, such as Euclid's axioms. In short, the managements of the new glamour-growth companies tend to favor business activities that lend themselves to careful study, experimentation, and control—the hard, practical realities of the lab, the shop, and the books.

What gets shortchanged are the realities of the *market*. Consumers are unpredictable, varied, fickle, stupid, shortsighted, stubborn, and generally bothersome. This is not what the engineer managers say, but deep down in their consciousness, it is what they believe. And this accounts for their concentration on what they know and what they can control—namely, product research, engineering, and production. The emphasis on production becomes particularly attractive when the product can be made at declining unit costs. There is no more inviting way of making money than by running the plant full blast.

The top-heavy science-engineering-production orientation of so many electronics companies works reasonably well today because they are pushing into new frontiers in which the armed services have pioneered virtually assured markets. The companies are in the felicitous position of having to fill, not find, markets, of not having to discover what the customer needs and wants but of having the customer voluntarily come forward with specific new product demands. If a team of consultants had been assigned specifically to design a business situation calculated to prevent the emergence and development of a customer-oriented marketing viewpoint, it could not have produced anything better than the conditions just described.

Stepchild Treatment. The oil industry is a stunning example of how science, technology, and mass production can divert an entire group of companies from their main task. To the extent the consumer is studied at all (which is not much), the focus is forever on getting information that is designed to help the oil companies improve what they are now doing. They try to discover more convincing advertising themes, more effective sales promotional drives, what the market shares of the various companies are, what people like or dislike about service station dealers and oil companies, and so forth. Nobody seems as interested in probing deeply into the basic human needs that the industry might be trying to satisfy as in probing into the basic properties of the raw material that the companies work with in trying to deliver customer satisfactions.

Basic questions about customers and markets seldom get asked. The latter occupy a stepchild status. They are recognized as existing, as having to be taken care of, but not worth very much real thought or dedicated attention. No oil company gets as excited about the customers in its own backyard as about the oil in the Sahara Desert. Nothing illustrates better the neglect of marketing than its treatment in the industry press.

The centennial issue of the *American Petroleum Institute Quarterly*, published in 1959 to celebrate the discovery of oil in Titusville, Pennsylvania, contained 21 feature articles proclaiming the industry's greatness. Only one of these talked about its achievements in marketing, and that was only a pictorial record of how service station architecture has changed. The issue also contained a special section on "New Horizons," which was devoted to showing the magnificent role oil would play in America's future. Every reference was ebulliently optimistic, never implying once that oil might have some hard competition. Even the reference to atomic energy was a cheerful catalog of how oil would help make atomic energy a success. There was not a single apprehension that the oil industry's affluence might be threatened or a suggestion that one "new horizon" might include new and better ways of serving oil's present customers.

But the most revealing example of the stepchild treatment that marketing gets is still another special series of short articles on "The Revolutionary Potential of Electronics." Under that heading, this list of articles appeared in the table of contents:

- "In the Search for Oil"
- "In Production Operations"
- "In Refinery Processes"
- "In Pipeline Operations"

Significantly, every one of the industry's major functional areas is listed, *except* marketing. Why? Either it is believed that electronics holds no revolutionary potential for petroleum marketing (which is palpably wrong), or the editors forgot to discuss marketing (which is more likely and illustrates its stepchild status).

The order in which the four functional areas are listed also betrays the alienation of the oil industry from the consumer. The industry is implicitly defined as beginning with the search for oil and ending with its distribution from the refinery. But the truth is, it seems to me, that the industry begins with the needs of the customer for its products. From that primal position its definition moves steadily back stream to areas of progressively lesser importance until it finally comes to rest at the search for oil.

The Beginning and End. The view that an industry is a customer-satisfying process, not a goods-producing process, is vital for all businesspeople to understand. An industry begins with the customer and his or her needs, not with a patent, a raw material, or a selling skill. Given the customer's needs, the industry develops backwards, first concerning itself with the physical *delivery* of customer satisfactions. Then it moves back further to *creating* the things by which these satisfactions are in part achieved. How these materials are created is a matter of indifference to the customer, hence the particular form of manufacturing, processing, or what have you cannot be considered as a vital aspect of the industry. Finally, the industry moves back still further to *finding* the raw materials necessary for making its products.

The irony of some industries oriented toward technical research and development is that the scientists who occupy the high executive positions are totally unscientific when it comes to defining their companies' overall needs and purposes. They violate the first two rules of the scientific method: being aware of and defining their companies' problems and then developing testable hypotheses about solving them. They are scientific only about the convenient things, such as laboratory and product experiments.

The customer (and the satisfaction of his or her deepest needs) is not considered to be "the problem"—not because there is any certain belief that no such problem exists but because an organizational lifetime has conditioned management to look in the opposite direction. Marketing is a stepchild.

I do not mean that selling is ignored. Far from it. But selling, again, is not marketing. As already pointed out, selling concerns itself with the tricks and techniques of getting people to exchange their cash for your product. It is not concerned with the values that the exchange is all about. And it does not, as marketing invariably does, view the entire business process as consisting of a tightly integrated effort to discover, create, arouse, and satisfy customer needs. The customer is somebody "out there" who, with proper cunning, can be separated from his or her loose change.

Actually, not even selling gets much attention in some technologically minded firms. Because there is a virtually guaranteed market for the abundant flow of their new products, they do not actually know what a real market is. It is as if they lived in a planned economy, moving their products routinely from factory to retail outlet. Their successful concentration on products tends to convince them of the soundness of what they have been doing, and they fail to see the gathering clouds over the market.

•••

Less than 75 years ago, American railroads enjoyed a fierce loyalty among astute Wall Streeters. European monarchs invested in them heavily. Eternal wealth was thought to be the benediction for anybody who could scrape together a few thousand dollars to put into rail stocks. No other form of transportation could compete with the railroads in speed, flexibility, durability, economy, and growth potentials.

As Jacques Barzun put it, "By the turn of the century it was an institution, an image of man, a tradition, a code of honor, a source of poetry, a nursery of boyhood desires, a sublimest of toys, and the most solemn machine—next to the funeral hearse—that marks the epochs in man's life."[6]

Even after the advent of automobiles, trucks, and airplanes, the railroad tycoons remained imperturbably self-confident. If you had told them 60 years ago that in 30 years they would be flat on their backs, broke, and pleading for government subsidies, they would have thought you totally demented. Such a future was simply not considered possible. It was not even a discussable subject, or an askable question, or a matter that any sane person would consider worth speculating about. Yet a lot of "insane" notions now have matter-of-fact acceptance—for example, the idea of 100-ton tubes of metal moving smoothly through the air 20,000 feet above the earth, loaded with 100 sane and solid citizens casually drinking martinis—and they have dealt cruel blows to the railroads.

What specifically must other companies do to avoid this fate? What does customer orientation involve? These questions have in part been answered by the preceding examples and analysis. It would take another article to show in detail what is required for specific industries. In any case, it should be obvious that building an effective customer-oriented company involves far more than good intentions or promotional tricks; it involves profound matters of human organization and leadership. For the present, let me merely suggest what appear to be some general requirements.

The Visceral Feel of Greatness. Obviously, the company has to do what survival demands. It has to adapt to the requirements of the market, and it has to do it sooner rather than later. But mere survival is a so-so aspiration. Anybody can survive in some way or other, even the skid row bum. The trick is to survive gallantly, to feel the surging impulse of commercial mastery: not just to experience the sweet smell of success but to have the visceral feel of entrepreneurial greatness.

No organization can achieve greatness without a vigorous leader who is driven onward by a pulsating *will to succeed*. A leader has to have a vision of grandeur, a vision that can produce eager followers in vast numbers. In business, the followers are the customers.

In order to produce these customers, the entire corporation must be viewed as a customer-creating and customer-satisfying organism. Management must think of itself not as producing products but as providing customer-creating value satisfactions. It must push this idea (and everything it means and requires) into every nook and cranny of the organization. It has to do this continuously and with the kind of flair that excites and stimulates the people in it. Otherwise, the company will be merely a series of pigeonholed parts, with no consolidating sense of purpose or direction.

In short, the organization must learn to think of itself not as producing goods or services but as *buying customers*, as doing the things that will make people *want* to do business with it. And the chief executive has the inescapable responsibility for creating this environment, this viewpoint, this attitude, this aspiration. The chief executive must set the company's style, its direction, and its goals. This means knowing precisely where he or she wants to go and making sure the whole organization is enthusiastically aware of where that is. This is a first requisite of leadership, for *unless a leader knows where he is going, any road will take him there.*

If any road is okay, the chief executive might as well pack his attaché case and go fishing. If an organization does not know or care where it is going, it does not need to advertise that fact with a ceremonial figurehead. Everybody will notice it soon enough.

1. Jacques Barzun, "Trains and the Mind of Man," *Holiday*, February 1960.
2. For more details, see M.M. Zimmerman, *The Super Market: A Revolution in Distribution* (McGraw-Hill, 1955).
3. Ibid., pp. 45–47.
4. John Kenneth Galbraith, *The Affluent Society* (Houghton Mifflin, 1958).
5. Henry Ford, *My Life and Work* (Doubleday, 1923).
6. Barzun, "Trains and the Mind of Man."

Reprint R0407L
Harvard Business Review OnPoint 7243
To order, see the next page
or call 800-988-0886 or 617-783-7500
or go to www.hbr.org

Harvard Business Review OnPoint articles enhance the full-text article with a summary of its key points and a selection of its company examples to help you quickly absorb and apply the concepts. Harvard Business Review OnPoint collections include three OnPoint articles and an overview comparing the various perspectives on a specific topic.

Further Reading

Marketing Myopia is also part of the Harvard Business Review OnPoint collection **Create–Then Dominate–New Markets,** Product no. 7235, which includes these additional articles:

Creating New Market Space
W. Chan Kim and Renée A. Mauborgne
Harvard Business Review
July 2004
Product no. 726X

Value Innovation: The Strategic Logic of High Growth
W. Chan Kim and Renée A. Mauborgne
Harvard Business Review
July 2004
Product no. 7251

Harvard Business Review

To Order

For reprints, Harvard Business Review OnPoint orders, and subscriptions to Harvard Business Review:
Call 800-988-0886 or 617-783-7500.
Go to www.hbr.org

For customized and quantity orders of reprints and Harvard Business Review OnPoint products:
Call Frank Tamoshunas at
617-783-7626,
or e-mail him at
ftamoshunas@hbsp.harvard.edu

PAGE 15

Essential Reading 2

'How competitive forces shape strategy' by Michael E. Porter is on the next page

(Source: Porter, M.E., 1990, 'How competitive forces shape strategy', *Harvard Business Review,* Vol.57, No.2, pp.137-45.)

JULY-AUGUST 1997

How Competitive Forces Shape Strategy

Awareness of these forces can help a company stake out a position in its industry that is less vulnerable to attack

by Michael E. Porter

The essence of strategy formulation is coping with competition. Yet it is easy to view competition too narrowly and too pessimistically. While one sometimes hears executives complaining to the contrary, intense competition in an industry is neither coincidence nor bad luck.

Moreover, in the fight for market share, competition is not manifested only in the other players. Rather, competition in an industry is rooted in its underlying economics, and competitive forces exist that go well beyond the established combatants in a particular industry. Customers, suppliers, potential entrants, and substitute products are all competitors that may be more or less prominent or active depending on the industry.

The state of competition in an industry depends on five basic forces, which are diagrammed in the *Exhibit* on page 6. The collective strength of these forces determines the ultimate profit potential of an industry. It ranges from *intense* in industries like tires, metal cans, and steel, where no company earns spectacular returns on investment, to *mild* in industries like oil field services and equipment, soft drinks, and toiletries, where there is room for quite high returns.

In the economists' "perfectly competitive" industry, jockeying for position is unbridled and entry to the industry very easy. This kind of industry structure, of course, offers the worst prospect for long-run profitability. The weaker the forces collectively, however, the greater the opportunity for superior performance.

Mr. Porter is a specialist in industrial economics and business strategy. An associate professor of business administration at the Harvard Business School, he has created a course there entitled "Industry and Competitive Analysis." He sits on the boards of three companies and consults on strategy matters, and he has written many articles for economics journals and published two books. One of them, Interbrand Choice, Strategy and Bilateral Market Power *(Harvard University Press, 1976) is an out-growth of his doctoral thesis, for which he won the coveted Wells prize awarded by the Harvard economics department. He has recently completed two book manuscripts, one on competitive analysis in industry and the other (written with Michael Spence and Richard Caves) on competition in the open economy.*

HARVARD BUSINESS REVIEW March-April 1979

Whatever their collective strength, the corporate strategist's goal is to find a position in the industry where his or her company can best defend itself against these forces or can influence them in its favor. The collective strength of the forces may be painfully apparent to all the antagonists; but to cope with them, the strategist must delve below the surface and analyze the sources of each. For example, what makes the industry vulnerable to entry, What determines the bargaining power of suppliers?

Knowledge of these underlying sources of competitive pressure provides the groundwork for a strategic agenda of action. They highlight the critical strengths and weaknesses of the company, animate the positioning of the company in its industry, clarify the areas where strategic changes may yield the greatest payoff, and highlight the places where industry trends promise to hold the greatest significance as either opportunities or threats. Understanding these sources also proves to be of help in considering areas for diversification.

Contending forces

The strongest competitive force or forces determine the profitability of an industry and so are of greatest importance in strategy formulation. For example, even a company with a strong position in an industry unthreatened by potential entrants will earn low returns if it faces a superior or a lower-cost substitute product—as the leading manufacturers of vacuum tubes and coffee percolators have learned to their sorrow. In such a situation, coping with the substitute product becomes the number one strategic priority.

Different forces take on prominence, of course, in shaping competition in each industry. In the ocean-going tanker industry the key force is probably the buyers (the major oil companies), while in tires it is powerful OEM buyers coupled with tough competitors. In the steel industry the key forces are foreign competitors and substitute materials.

Every industry has an underlying structure, or a set of fundamental economic and technical characteristics, that gives rise to these competitive forces. The strategist, wanting to position his or her company to cope best with its industry environment or to influence that environment in the company's favor, must learn what makes the environment tick.

This view of competition pertains equally to industries dealing in services and to those selling products. To avoid monotony in this article, I refer to both products and services as "products." The same general principles apply to all types of business.

A few characteristics are critical to the strength of each competitive force. I shall discuss them in this section.

Threat of entry

New entrants to an industry bring new capacity, the desire to gain market share, and often substantial resources. Companies diversifying through acquisition into the industry from other markets often leverage their resources to cause a shake-up, as Philip Morris did with Miller beer.

The seriousness of the threat of entry depends on the barriers present and on the reaction from existing competitors that entrants can expect. If barriers to entry are high and newcomers can expect sharp retaliation from the entrenched competitors, obviously the newcomers will not pose a serious threat of entering.

There are six major sources of barriers to entry:

1. *Economies of scale*—These economies deter entry by forcing the aspirant either to come in on a large scale or to accept a cost disadvantage. Scale economies in production, research, marketing, and service are probably the key barriers to entry in the mainframe computer industry, as Xerox and GE sadly discovered. Economies of scale can also act as hurdles in distribution, utilization of the sales force, financing, and nearly any other part of a business.

2. *Product differentiation*—Brand identification creates a barrier by forcing entrants to spend heavily to overcome customer loyalty. Advertising, customer service, being first in the industry, and product differences are among the factors fostering brand identification. It is perhaps the most important entry barrier in soft drinks, over-the-counter drugs, cosmetics, investment banking, and public accounting. To create high fences around their businesses, brewers couple brand identification with economies of scale in production, distribution, and marketing.

3. *Capital requirements*—The need to invest large financial resources in order to compete creates a barrier to entry, particularly if the capital is required for unrecoverable expenditures in up-front advertising or R&D. Capital is necessary not only for fixed facilities but also for customer credit, inventories, and absorbing start-up losses. While major corporations have the financial resources to invade almost any industry, the huge capital requirements in certain fields, such as computer manufacturing and mineral extraction, limit the pool of likely entrants.

4. *Cost disadvantages independent of size*—Entrenched companies may have cost advantages not

The Experience Curve as an Entry Barrier

In recent years, the experience curve has become widely discussed as a key element of industry structure. According to this concept, unit costs in many manufacturing industries (some dogmatic adherents say in *all* manufacturing industries) as well as in some service industries decline with "experience," or a particular company's cumulative volume of production. (The experience curve, which encompasses many factors, is a broader concept than the better known learning curve, which refers to the efficiency achieved over a period of time by workers through much repetition.)

The causes of the decline in unit costs are a combination of elements, including economies of scale, the learning curve for labor, and capital-labor substitution. The cost decline creates a barrier to entry because new competitors with no "experience" face higher costs than established ones, particularly the producer with the largest market share, and have difficulty catching up with the entrenched competitors.

Adherents of the experience curve concept stress the importance of achieving market leadership to maximize this barrier to entry, and they recommend aggressive action to achieve it, such as price cutting in anticipation of falling costs in order to build volume. For the combatant that cannot achieve a healthy market share, the prescription is usually, "Get out."

Is the experience curve an entry barrier on which strategies should be built? The answer is: not in every industry. In fact, in some industries, building a strategy on the experience curve can be potentially disastrous. That costs decline with experience in some industries is not news to corporate executives. The significance of the experience curve for strategy depends on what factors are causing the decline.

If costs are falling because a growing company can reap economies of scale through more efficient, automated facilities and vertical integration, then the cumulative volume of production is unimportant to its relative cost position. Here the lowest-cost producer is the one with the largest, most efficient facilities.

A new entrant may well be more efficient than the more experienced competitors; if it has built the newest plant, it will face no disadvantage in having to catch up. The strategic prescription, "You must have the largest, most efficient plant," is a lot different from, "You must produce the greatest cumulative output of the item to get your costs down."

Whether a drop in costs with cumulative (not absolute) volume erects an entry barrier also depends on the sources of the decline. If costs go down because of technical advances known generally in the industry or because of the development of improved equipment that can be copied or purchased from equipment suppliers, the experience curve is no entry barrier at all – in fact, new or less experienced competitors may actually enjoy a cost *advantage* over the leaders. Free of the legacy of heavy past investments, the newcomer or less experienced competitor can purchase or copy the newest and lowest-cost equipment and technology.

If, however, experience can be kept proprietary, the leaders will maintain a cost advantage. But new entrants may require less experience to reduce their costs than the leaders needed. All this suggests that the experience curve can be a shaky entry barrier on which to build a strategy.

While space does not permit a complete treatment here, I want to mention a few other crucial elements in determining the appropriateness of a strategy built on the entry barrier provided by the experience curve:

☐ The height of the barrier depends on how important costs are to competition compared with other areas like marketing, selling, and innovation.

☐ The barrier can be nullified by product or process innovations leading to a substantially new technology and thereby creating an entirely new experience curve.* New entrants can leapfrog the industry leaders and alight on the new experience curve, to which those leaders may be poorly positioned to jump.

☐ If more than one strong company is building its strategy on the experience curve, the consequences can be nearly fatal. By the time only one rival is left pursuing such a strategy, industry growth may have stopped and the prospects of reaping the spoils of victory long since evaporated.

---

*For an example drawn from the history of the automobile industry see William J. Abernathy and Kenneth Wayne, "The Limits of the Learning Curve," HBR September/October 1974, p.109.

---

available to potential rivals, no matter what their size and attainable economies of scale. These advantages can stem from the effects of the learning curve (and of its first cousin, the experience curve), proprietary technology, access to the best raw materials sources, assets purchased at preinflation prices, government subsidies, or favorable locations. Sometimes cost advantages are legally enforceable, as they are through patents. (For an analysis of the much-discussed experience curve as a barrier to entry, see the ruled insert above.)

5. *Access to distribution channels*—The newcomer on the block must, of course, secure distribution of its product or service. A new food product, for example, must displace others from the supermarket shelf via price breaks, promotions, intense

selling efforts, or some other means. The more limited the wholesale or retail channels are and the more that existing competitors have these tied up, obviously the tougher that entry into the industry will be. Sometimes this barrier is so high that, to surmount it, a new contestant must create its own distribution channels, as Timex did in the watch industry in the 1950s.

6. *Government policy*—The government can limit or even foreclose entry to industries with such controls as license requirements and limits on access to raw materials. Regulated industries like trucking, liquor retailing, and freight forwarding are noticeable examples; more subtle government restrictions operate in fields like ski-area development and coal mining. The government also can play a major indirect role by affecting entry barriers through controls such as air and water pollution standards and safety regulations.

The potential rival's expectations about the reaction of existing competitors also will influence its decision on whether to enter. The company is likely to have second thoughts if incumbents have previously lashed out at new entrants or if:

☐ The incumbents possess substantial resources to fight back, including excess cash and unused borrowing power, productive capacity, or clout with distribution channels and customers.

☐ The incumbents seem likely to cut prices because of a desire to keep market shares or because of industrywide excess capacity.

☐ Industry growth is slow, affecting its ability to absorb the new arrival and probably causing the financial performance of all the parties involved to decline.

Changing conditions

From a strategic standpoint there are two important additional points to note about the threat of entry.

First, it changes, of course, as these conditions change. The expiration of Polaroid's basic patents on instant photography, for instance, greatly reduced its absolute cost entry barrier built by proprietary technology. It is not surprising that Kodak plunged into the market. Product differentiation in printing has all but disappeared. Conversely, in the auto industry economies of scale increased enormously with post-World War II automation and vertical integration—virtually stopping successful new entry.

Second, strategic decisions involving a large segment of an industry can have a major impact on the conditions determining the threat of entry. For example, the actions of many U.S. wine producers in the 1960s to step up product introductions, raise advertising levels, and expand distribution nationally surely strengthened the entry roadblocks by raising economies of scale and making access to distribution channels more difficult. Similarly, decisions by members of the recreational vehicle industry to vertically integrate in order to lower costs have greatly increased the economies of scale and raised the capital cost barriers.

Powerful suppliers & buyers

Suppliers can exert bargaining power on participants in an industry by raising prices or reducing the quality of purchased goods and services. Powerful suppliers can thereby squeeze profitability out of an industry unable to recover cost increases in its own prices. By raising their prices, soft drink concentrate producers have contributed to the erosion of profitability of bottling companies because the bottlers, facing intense competition from powdered mixes, fruit drinks, and other beverages, have limited freedom to raise *their* prices accordingly. Customers likewise can force down prices, demand higher quality or more service, and play competitors off against each other—all at the expense of industry profits.

The power of each important supplier or buyer group depends on a number of characteristics of its market situation and on the relative importance of its sales or purchases to the industry compared with its overall business.

A *supplier* group is powerful if:

☐ It is dominated by a few companies and is more concentrated than the industry it sells to.

☐ Its product is unique or at least differentiated, or if it has built up switching costs. Switching costs are fixed costs buyers face in changing suppliers. These arise because, among other things, a buyer's product specifications tie it to particular suppliers, it has invested heavily in specialized ancillary equipment or in reaming how to operate a supplier's equipment (as in computer software), or its production lines are connected to the supplier's manufacturing facilities (as in some manufacture of beverage containers).

☐ It is not obliged to contend with other products for sale to the industry. For instance, the competition between the steel companies and the aluminum companies to sell to the can industry checks the power of each supplier.

☐ It poses a credible threat of integrating forward into the industry's business. This provides a check against the industry's ability to improve the terms on which it purchases.

☐ The industry is not an important customer of the supplier group. If the industry is an important customer, suppliers' fortunes will be closely tied to the industry, and they will want to protect the industry through reasonable pricing and assistance in activities like R&D and lobbying.

A *buyer* group is powerful if:

☐ It is concentrated or purchases in large volumes. Large volume buyers are particularly potent forces if heavy fixed costs characterize the industry—as they do in metal containers, corn refining, and bulk chemicals, for example—which raise the stakes to keep capacity filled.

☐ The products it purchases from the industry are standard or undifferentiated. The buyers, sure that they can always find alternative suppliers, may play one company against another, as they do in aluminum extrusion.

☐ The products it purchases from the industry form a component of its product and represent a significant fraction of its cost. The buyers are likely to shop for a favorable price and purchase selectively. Where the product sold by the industry in question is a small fraction of buyers' costs, buyers are usually much less price sensitive.

☐ It earns low profits, which create great incentive to lower its purchasing costs. Highly profitable buyers, however, are generally less price sensitive (that is, of course, if the item does not represent a large fraction of their costs).

☐ The industry's product is unimportant to the quality of the buyers' products or services. Where the quality of the buyers' products is very much affected by the industry's product, buyers are generally less price sensitive. Industries in which this situation obtains include oil field equipment, where a malfunction can lead to large losses, and enclosures for electronic medical and test instruments, where the quality of the enclosure can influence the user's impression about the quality of the equipment inside.

☐ The industry's product does not save the buyer money. Where the industry's product or service can pay for itself many times over, the buyer is rarely price sensitive; rather, he is interested in quality. This is true in services like investment banking and public accounting, where errors in judgment can be costly and embarrassing, and in businesses like the logging of oil wells, where an accurate survey can save thousands of dollars in drilling costs.

☐ The buyers pose a credible threat of integrating backward to make the industry's product. The Big Three auto producers and major buyers of cars have often used the threat of self-manufacture as a bar-

Exhibit
Forces governing competition in an industry

Threat of new entrants

Bargaining power of suppliers

The industry
Jockeying for position among current competitors

Bargaining power of customers

Threat of substitute products or services

gaining lever. But sometimes an industry engenders a threat to buyers that its members may integrate forward.

Most of these sources of buyer power can be attributed to consumers as a group as well as to industrial and commercial buyers; only a modification of the frame of reference is necessary. Consumers tend to be more price sensitive if they are purchasing products that are undifferentiated, expensive relative to their incomes, and of a sort where quality is not particularly important.

The buying power of retailers is determined by the same rules, with one important addition. Retailers can gain significant bargaining power over manufacturers when they can influence consumers' purchasing decisions, as they do in audio components, jewelry, appliances, sporting goods, and other goods.

Strategic action

A company's choice of suppliers to buy from or buyer groups to sell to should be viewed as a crucial strategic decision. A company can improve its strategic posture by finding suppliers or buyers who possess the least power to influence it adversely.

Most common is the situation of a company being able to choose whom it will sell to—in other words, buyer selection. Rarely do all the buyer groups a company sells to enjoy equal power. Even

6

if a company sells to a single industry, segments usually exist within that industry that exercise less power (and that are therefore less price sensitive) than others. For example, the replacement market for most products is less price sensitive than the overall market.

As a rule, a company can sell to powerful buyers and still come away with above-average profitability only if it is a low-cost producer in its industry or if its product enjoys some unusual, if not unique, features. In supplying large customers with electric motors, Emerson Electric earns high returns because its low cost position permits the company to meet or undercut competitors' prices.

If the company lacks a low cost position or a unique product, selling to everyone is self-defeating because the more sales it achieves, the more vulnerable it becomes. The company may have to muster the courage to turn away business and sell only to less potent customers.

Buyer selection has been a key to the success of National Can and Crown Cork & Seal. They focus on the segments of the can industry where they can create product differentiation, minimize the threat of backward integration, and otherwise mitigate the awesome power of their customers. Of course, some industries do not enjoy the luxury of selecting "good" buyers.

As the factors creating supplier and buyer power change with time or as a result of a company's strategic decisions, naturally the power of these groups rises or declines. In the ready-to-wear clothing industry, as the buyers (department stores and clothing stores) have become more concentrated and control has passed to large chains, the industry has come under increasing pressure and suffered falling margins. The industry has been unable to differentiate its product or engender switching costs that lock in its buyers enough to neutralize these trends.

Substitute products

By placing a ceiling on prices it can charge, substitute products or services limit the potential of an industry. Unless it can upgrade the quality of the product or differentiate it somehow (as via marketing), the industry will suffer in earnings and possibly in growth.

Manifestly, the more attractive the price-performance trade-off offered by substitute products, the firmer the lid placed on the industry's profit potential. Sugar producers confronted with the large-scale commercialization of high-fructose corn syrup, a sugar substitute, are learning this lesson today.

Substitutes not only limit profits in normal times; they also reduce the bonanza an industry can reap in boom times. In 1978 the producers of fiberglass insulation enjoyed unprecedented demand as a result of high energy costs and severe winter weather. But the industry's ability to raise prices was tempered by the plethora of insulation substitutes, including cellulose, rock wool, and styrofoam. These substitutes are bound to become an even stronger force once the current round of plant additions by fiberglass insulation producers has boosted capacity enough to meet demand (and then some).

Substitute products that deserve the most attention strategically are those that (a) are subject to trends improving their price-performance trade-off with the industry's product, or (b) are produced by industries earning high profits. Substitutes often come rapidly into play if some development increases competition in their industries and causes price reduction or performance improvement.

Jockeying for position

Rivalry among existing competitors takes the familiar form of jockeying for position—using tactics like price competition, product introduction, and advertising slugfests. Intense rivalry is related to the presence of a number of factors:

□ Competitors are numerous or are roughly equal in size and power. In many U.S. industries in recent years foreign contenders, of course, have become part of the competitive picture.

□ Industry growth is slow, precipitating fights for market share that involve expansion-minded members.

□ The product or service lacks differentiation or switching costs, which lock in buyers and protect one combatant from raids on its customers by another.

□ Fixed costs are high or the product is perishable, creating strong temptation to cut prices. Many basic materials businesses, like paper and aluminum, suffer from this problem when demand slackens.

□ Capacity is normally augmented in large increments. Such additions, as in the chlorine and vinyl chloride businesses, disrupt the industry's supply-demand balance and often lead to periods of overcapacity and price cutting.

□ Exit barriers are high. Exit barriers, like very specialized assets or management's loyalty to a particular business, keep companies competing even though they may be earning low or even negative returns on investment. Excess capacity remains functioning, and the profitability of the healthy competitors suffers as the sick ones hang on.[1] If the entire industry suffers from overcapacity, it may seek government help—particularly if foreign competition is present.

☐ The rivals are diverse in strategies, origins, and "personalities." They have different ideas about how to compete and continually run head-on into each other in the process.

As an industry matures, its growth rate changes, resulting in declining profits and (often) a shakeout. In the booming recreational vehicle industry of the early 1970s, nearly every producer did well; but slow growth since then has eliminated the high returns, except for the strongest members, not to mention many of the weaker companies. The same profit story has been played out in industry after industry—snowmobiles, aerosol packaging, and sports equipment are just a few examples.

An acquisition can introduce a very different personality to an industry, as has been the case with Black & Decker's takeover of McCullough, the producer of chain saws. Technological innovation can boost the level of fixed costs in the production process, as it did in the shift from batch to continuous-line photo finishing in the 1960s.

While a company must live with many of these factors—because they are built into industry economics—it may have some latitude for improving matters through strategic shifts. For example, it may try to raise buyers' switching costs or increase product differentiation. A focus on selling efforts in the fastest-growing segments of the industry or on market areas with the lowest fixed costs can reduce the impact of industry rivalry. If it is feasible, a company can try to avoid confrontation with competitors having high exit barriers and can thus sidestep involvement in bitter price cutting.

Formulation of strategy

Once having assessed the forces affecting competition in an industry and their underlying causes, the corporate strategist can identify the company's strengths and weaknesses. The crucial strengths and weaknesses from a strategic standpoint are the company's posture vis-à-vis the underlying causes of each force. Where does it stand against substitutes? Against the sources of enery barriers?

Then the strategist can devise a plan of action that may include (1) positioning the company so that its capabilities provide the best defense against the competitive force; and/or (2) influencing the balance of the forces through strategic moves, thereby improving the company's position; and/or (3) anticipating shifts in the factors underlying the

forces and responding to them, with the hope of exploiting change by choosing a strategy appropriate for the new competitive balance before opponents recognize it. I shall consider each strategic approach in turn.

Positioning the company

The first approach takes the structure of the industry as given and matches the company's strengths and weaknesses to it. Strategy can be viewed as building defenses against the competitive forces or as finding positions in the industry where the forces are weakest.

Knowledge of the company's capabilities and of the causes of the competitive forces will highlight the areas where the company should confront competition and where avoid it. If the company is a low-cost producer, it may choose to confront powerful buyers while it takes care to sell them only products not vulnerable to competition from substitutes.

The success of Dr Pepper in the soft drink industry illustrates the coupling of realistic knowledge of corporate strengths with sound industry analysis to yield a superior strategy. Coca-Cola and PepsiCola dominate Dr Pepper's industry, where many small concentrate producers compete for a piece of the action. Dr Pepper chose a strategy of avoiding the largest-selling drink segment, maintaining a narrow flavor line, forgoing the development of a captive bottler network, and marketing heavily. The company positioned itself so as to be least vulnerable to its competitive forces while it exploited its small size.

In the $11.5 billion soft drink industry, barriers to entry in the form of brand identification, large-scale marketing, and access to a bottler network are enormous. Rather than accept the formidable costs and scale economies in having its own bottler network—that is, following the lead of the Big Two and of Seven-Up—Dr Pepper took advantage of the different flavor of its drink to "piggyback" on Coke and Pepsi bottlers who wanted a full line to sell to customers. Dr Pepper coped with the power of these buyers through extraordinary service and other efforts to distinguish its treatment of them from that of Coke and Pepsi.

Many small companies in the soft drink business offer cola drinks that thrust them into head-to-head competition against the majors. Dr Pepper, however, maximized product differentiation by maintaining a narrow line of beverages built around an unusual flavor.

Finally, Dr Pepper met Coke and Pepsi with an advertising onslaught emphasizing the alleged uniqueness of its single flavor. This campaign built strong brand identification and great customer loyalty. Helping its efforts was the fact that Dr Pepper's formula involved lower raw materials cost, which gave the company an absolute cost advantage over its major competitors.

There are no economies of scale in soft drink concentrate production, so Dr Pepper could prosper despite its small share of the business (6%). Thus Dr Pepper confronted competition in marketing but avoided it in product line and in distribution. This artful positioning combined with good implementation has led to an enviable record in earnings and in the stock market.

Influencing the balance

When dealing with the forces that drive industry competition, a company can devise a strategy that takes the offensive. This posture is designed to do more than merely cope with the forces themselves; it is meant to alter their causes.

Innovations in marketing can raise brand identification or otherwise differentiate the product. Capital investments in large-scale facilities or vertical integration affect entry barriers. The balance of forces is partly a result of external factors and partly in the company's control.

Exploiting industry change

Industry evolution is important strategically because evolution, of course, brings with it changes in the sources of competition I have identified. In the familiar product life-cycle pattern, for example, growth rates change, product differentiation is said to decline as the business becomes more mature, and the companies tend to integrate vertically.

These trends are not so important in themselves; what is critical is whether they affect the sources of competition. Consider vertical integration. In the maturing minicomputer industry, extensive vertical integration, both in manufacturing and in software development, is taking place. This very significant trend is greatly raising economies of scale as well as the amount of capital necessary to compete in the industry. This in turn is raising barriers to entry and may drive some smaller competitors out of the industry once growth levels off.

Obviously, the trends carrying the highest priority from a strategic standpoint are those that affect the most important sources of competition in the industry and those that elevate new causes to the forefront. In contract aerosol packaging, for example, the trend toward less product differentiation is now dominant. It has increased buyers' power, lowered the barriers to entry, and intensified competi-

tion.

The framework for analyzing competition that I have described can also be used to predict the eventual profitability of an industry. In long-range planning the task is to examine each competitive force, forecast the magnitude of each underlying cause, and then construct a composite picture of the likely profit potential of the industry.

The outcome of such an exercise may differ a great deal from the existing industry structure. Today, for example, the solar heating business is populated by dozens and perhaps hundreds of companies, none with a major market position. Entry is easy, and competitors are battling to establish solar heating as a superior substitute for conventional methods.

The potential of this industry will depend largely on the shape of future barriers to entry, the improvement of the industry's position relative to substitutes, the ultimate intensity of competition, and the power captured by buyers and suppliers. These characteristics will in turn be influenced by such factors as the establishment of brand identities, significant economies of scale or experience curves in equipment manufacture wrought by technological change, the ultimate capital costs to compete, and the extent of overhead in production facilities.

The framework for analyzing industry competition has direct benefits in setting diversification strategy. It provides a road map for answering the extremely difficult question inherent in diversification decisions: "What is the potential of this business?" Combining the framework with judgment in its application, a company may be able to spot an industry with a good future before this good future is reflected in the prices of acquisition candidates.

Multifaceted rivalry

Corporate managers have directed a great deal of attention to defining their businesses as a crucial step in strategy formulation. Theodore Levitt, in his classic 1960 article in HBR, argued strongly for avoiding the myopia of narrow, product-oriented industry definition.[2] Numerous other authorities have also stressed the need to look beyond product to function in defining a business, beyond national boundaries to potential international competition, and beyond the ranks of one's competitors today to those that may become competitors tomorrow. As a result of these urgings, the proper definition of a company's industry or industries has become an endlessly debated subject.

One motive behind this debate is the desire to exploit new markets. Another, perhaps more important motive is the fear of overlooking latent sources of competition that someday may threaten the industry. Many managers concentrate so single-mindedly on their direct antagonists in the fight for market share that they fail to realize that they are also competing with their customers and their suppliers for bargaining power. Meanwhile, they also neglect to keep a wary eye out for new entrants to the contest or fail to recognize the subtle threat of substitute products.

The key to growth—even survival—is to stake out a position that is less vulnerable to attack from head-to-head opponents, whether established or new, and less vulnerable to erosion from the direction of buyers, suppliers, and substitute goods. Establishing such a position can take many forms—solidifying relationships with favorable customers, differentiating the product either substantively or psychologically through marketing, integrating forward or backward, establishing technological leadership.

[1] *For a more complete discussion of exit barriers and their implications for strategy, see my article, "Please Note Location of Nearest Exit," California Management Review, Winter 1976, p. 21.*

[2] *Theodore Levitt, "Marketing Myopia," reprinted as an HBR Classic, September-October 1975, p. 26.*

Reprint 79208   To place an order, call 800-988-0886.

Essential Reading 3

Consumers and business ethics

Introduction

Consumers are obviously one of the most important stakeholders for any organization, since without the support of customers of some sort, such as through the demand for or purchase of goods and services, most organizations would be unlikely to survive for very long. By consumers, though, we do not just mean the end consumers who ultimately buy finished products in the shops, but also all of the organizations that purchase or otherwise contract for the provision of goods and services from other organizations. Your university, for example, is just as much a consumer as you or we are, in that it buys furniture, stationery, books, journals, cleaning services, and various other products and services in order to go about its business of providing teaching and research. It has also become increasingly common for people to refer to departments serviced in some way by other departments within the *same* organization as internal customers. Hence, consumers here should be regarded as a broad category including the whole chain of internal and external constituencies that receive goods or services of some kind, usually through some form of exchange.

Given the importance of consumer support for the ongoing success of an organization, it is no surprise that being ethical in dealing with consumers is generally regarded as one of the most crucial areas of business ethics. Moreover, since consumers are primarily outside the organization, ethical problems in this area are often some of the most visible and most difficult to hide of ethical violations. This can lead to potentially damaging public relations problems, media exposés, and other threats to the reputation of the corporation which might be more easily avoided in the context of employees, shareholders, and other stakeholders.

In this [reading], we shall examine the challenges faced by corporations in dealing ethically with consumers in the global economy. The main corporate functions responsible for dealing with consumers are sales and marketing, and it is evident that these professions have long been subjected to a great deal of ethical criticism. Many writers on marketing ethics have highlighted the lack of public trust in the advertising and sales professions (e.g. Laczniak and Murphy 1993; Assael 1995), and marketing is often argued to be perceived as the least ethical of all the business functions (Baumhart 1961; Tsalikis and Fritzsche 1989).

However, although ethics does not appear to have traditionally been a central concern of marketing professionals and academics, there is some evidence of moral considerations entering marketing thought for as long as marketing has existed as a distinct field in its own right (Desmond 1998). After all, it does not take someone with an MBA to work out that there are likely to be certain benefits in having customers that feel they have been treated honestly and ethically rather than just feeling like the victims of a cynical rip-off operation! More recently, though, there has been a surge in interest regarding ethical marketing, ethical consumption, and such issues, from both the public, practitioners, and academics alike. As we shall see, this has led to a fascinating, yet still unresolved debate about the nature of ethical marketing, and in particular about the role of consumers in shaping the social impact of corporations through their purchase decisions. In order to address such questions, though, we first have to establish the nature and scope of the stakeholder role played by consumers.

Consumers as stakeholders

It is by now largely commonplace to hear the argument that businesses are best served by treating their customers well. Indeed, this is essentially one of the core tenets of business strategy – that organizations succeed by outperforming their competitors in providing superior value to their customers. Those companies that prosper in the marketplace are those that pay close and continuous attention to satisfying their customers. Indeed, in many ways it is hard to argue against the logic of this argument. Of course, an organization will seek to satisfy its customers, for if it does not, then those customers will defect to competitors, thus resulting in loss of market share, and ultimately, profitability.

However, one might also ask why is it, if the interests of producers and consumers are so closely aligned, that ethical abuses of consumers continue to hit the headlines and that the reputation of the marketing and sales professions remains so poor? For example, in recent years, there have been numerous examples of firms being accused of treating their customers in a questionable manner:

- Tobacco companies have been accused of knowingly hooking their customers on a product hazardous to their health, whilst denying its addictive properties.
- Multinational drug companies have been accused of exploiting the sick and poor of the world by maintaining high prices for HIV treatments and preventing the sale of cheaper generic drugs in less developed countries.
- Football teams have been accused of exploiting the goodwill of their fans by continually changing their team strips in order to boost sales of expensive replica kits.
- Fashion brands and women's magazines have been accused of exacerbating eating disorders amongst their young readers by featuring idealized images of excessively thin models which only a minority of women can emulate in a physically and emotionally healthy manner.
- Rail, air, and automotive companies have been accused of putting their customers' lives at risk by compromising safety standards in the face of competitive pressures and cost-cutting exercises.
- Financial services companies have been accused of deliberately misleading their customers in order to enhance sales of insurance policies, pensions, and other personal finance products.

- Airlines have been accused of misleading their consumers about the real price of flights by omitting airport tax and other extras from the prices advertised in promotions.

These are just a few of the many examples that are regularly revealed by the media and by consumer groups and other 'watchdog' organizations. Clearly, such incidences are cause for concern, but what does this tell us about the nature of the stake held by consumers? The first point to make here is that we must question whether the satisfaction of consumer stakeholders is necessarily always consistent with the best interests of the firm. Whilst such an assumption of aligned interests may well be legitimate in some contexts, or where certain conditions are met, there may also be situations where the interests of buyers and sellers diverge (Smith 1995).

... [A]t the most basic level, the co-alignment of interests between the two groups depends on the availability of alternative choices that the consumer might reasonably be able to switch to. Secondly, though, in the absence of a clear mutual interest in all contexts, we also need a normative conception of the stake held by consumers in order to determine what constitutes (un) ethical behaviour towards them. Typically, this normative basis has been established on notions of consumer rights.

... [C]onsumer rights can be regarded as follows:

> Consumer rights rest upon the assumption that consumer dignity should be respected, and that producers have a duty to treat consumers as ends in themselves, and not only as means to the end of the producer. Thus, consumer rights are inalienable entitlements to fair treatment when entering into exchanges with other parties.

What constitutes fair treatment is, however, open to considerable debate. In the past, consumers were adjudged to have few if any clear rights in this respect, and the legal framework for market exchange was largely predicated on the notion of *caveat emptor*, or buyer beware (see Smith 1995). Under caveat emptor, the consumer's sole right was to veto purchase and decide not to purchase something (Boatright 2000: 273). The burden for protecting the consumer's interest should they have wanted to go ahead with purchase lay with the consumer themself, not with the party making the sale. Therefore, under the rule of buyer beware, providing producers abided by the law, it was the consumer's responsibility to show due diligence in avoiding questionable products. If they were subsequently harmed by or dissatisfied with a product or service, it was regarded as their own fault.

The limits of 'caveat emptor'

During the latter part of the twentieth century, this notion of caveat emptor was gradually eroded by changing societal expectations and the introduction of consumer protection laws in most developed countries (Smith 1995). Consequently, protection of various consumer rights, such as the right to safe and efficacious (i.e. effective in doing what they are supposed to do) products and the right to truthful measurements and labelling, are now enshrined in EU regulations as well as in the national and regional legal framework of member countries. … [B]usiness ethics often begins where the law ends. So, it is frequently in the context of the more ill-defined or questionable rights of consumers, and those that are not legally protected, that the most important ethical questions arise.

For example, we might reasonably suggest that consumers have a right to truthful information about products, and legislation usually proscribes the deliberate falsification of product information on packaging and in advertisements. However, certain claims made by manufacturers and advertisers might not be factually untrue, but may end up misleading consumers about potential benefits. For instance, in many European countries, claims that a food product is 'low fat' are permissible providing the product is lower in fat than an alternative, such as a competing product or another of the company's product line. This means that even a product with 80 per cent fat can be labelled 'low fat' providing the company also markets an alternative with 85 per cent fat. For customers seeking a healthy diet, the 'low fat' product may seem attractive, but might not actually provide the genuinely healthy benefits as suggested by the labelling. We might question then whether the consumer purchasing such a product has been treated fairly by the seller. It is in such grey areas of consumers' rights that questionable marketing practices arise. …

… [I]t is important to mention at this stage that the stake consumers hold in corporations does not only provide them with certain rights, but also entrusts them with certain responsibilities too. At one level, we can think of this just in terms of the expectations we might have for consumers themselves to act ethically in dealing with the producers of products. Customers might sometimes be in a position where they can take an unfair advantage of those who supply them with products, particularly if we think about the situation where customers are actually other firms. For instance, powerful retailers may exert excessive pressure on their suppliers in order to squeeze the lowest possible prices out of them for their products. Even at the level of individual consumers like you or us, there are certain expectations placed on us to desist from lying, stealing, or otherwise acting unethically in our dealings with retailers.

At a different level, though, and probably more importantly, various writers have also suggested that there are certain responsibilities placed on us as consumers for controlling corporations in some way, or for avoiding environmental problems, through our purchase decisions. If we don't like the way that Reebok treats its third world labour force, or the way that Exxon Mobil has responded to global warming, is it not also up to us to make a stand and avoid buying their products in order to get the message through? If we really want to achieve sustainability, don't we have to accept certain curbs on our own personal consumption? These are vital questions in the context of corporate citizenship and sustainability …

References

Assael, H. (1995). *Consumer Behaviour and Marketing Action,* 5th edn. Cincinnati: South-Western College.

Baumhart, R. C. (1961). 'How ethical are businesses?' *Harvard Business Review,* July-Aug.: 6.

Boatwright, J. R. (2000). *Ethics and the Conduct of Business*, 3rd edn. Upper Saddle River, NJ: Prentice Hall.

Desmond, J. (1998). 'Marketing and moral indifference'. In M. Parker (ed.), *Ethics and Organizations.* London: Sage: 173–96.

Laczniak, G. R., and Murphy, P. E. (1993). *Ethical Marketing Decisions: The Higher Road.* Boston: Allyn & Bacon.

Smith, N. C. (1995). 'Marketing strategies for the ethics era'. *Sloan Management Review*, 36/4: 85–97.

Tsalikis, J., and Fritzsche, D. J. (1989). 'Business ethics: a literature review with a focus on marketing ethics'. *Journal of Business Ethics*, 8: 695–743.

(Source: Crane, A. and Matten, D., 2003, *Business Ethics,* Oxford, Oxford University Press, pp. 265–9.)

Essential Reading 4

Societal adaptation: a new challenge for marketing

Is a marketing system that maximizes individual choice and stresses individual satisfaction anachronistic in a world with growing awareness of its limited environmental resources? The author believes marketing is about to undergo a profound change by shifting its emphasis to nonmaterial consumption and societal considerations. Several ways are suggested in which marketing might adapt to the changed circumstances brought about by environmental pressures.

American social institutions are currently experiencing a time of unrest. 'Business' and 'social responsibility,' formerly thought by many to be anathema, are increasingly being linked together, while universities are marked by the search for relevancy. In spite of the unsettling atmosphere, this self-examination and soul-searching by business and academic communities may be regarded as a healthy prelude to change. For in a dynamic environment, social institutions must either change or disappear as they become inappropriate to meet new conditions.

The marketing system is one such social institution. There have recently been several indications that it is about to undergo a profound change in response to environmental pressure. On the one hand, the marketing system is asked to provide, and is capable of delivering, goods which make the life of the individual consumer more comfortable and convenient. On the other hand, there are those who decry the adverse societal effects of both the production and consumption of many goods which play an important role in consumption. This presents a fundamental dilemma for the marketing system and a major challenge for those who use or depend on it.

However, it is not yet clear whether those having the most at stake in business and academia have recognized the basic questions that this problem raises with respect to the future of marketing. The reaction of businessmen has been diverse. Some, of course, have ignored the problem; others have directed their attention to an isolated aspect of it, for example, the development of disposable packaging, or have cynically exploited the issues for their own ends. An example of the latter is the exhortation of a cigarette manufacturer to 'stop smogging' by switching to his brand.

The degree of academic sensitivity to the problem has exhibited a similar variance. For instance, one prominent writer in the marketing field recently suggested that in the future a major function of marketing will be '... to justify and stimulate our age of consumption' by educating consumers to forsake the puritan ethic.[1]

In contrast, another has stated that a system which depends on the 'marketing concept' as a guide to marketing policy is outmoded because its application has led to the manufacture of such socially undesirable products as cigarettes, guns, and armaments. He suggested that the marketing concept be replaced by the 'human concept' which would still rely on need and profit, but which would also consider the human and environmental aspects of the decision.[2] It is significant, however, that the first writer failed to relate the advocacy of growth through consumption to its ultimate societal consequences, and the second made no effort to come to grips with either the difficulties inherent in the implementation of the human concept, or its consequent impact on the marketing system.

It is in their failure to explore the ultimate consequences that businessmen and marketing scholars have been deficient. The situation is one where individual needs appear to be limitless. At the same time, it is becoming apparent that the available resources are essentially finite. For example, material resources such as land, timber, and some minerals are becoming scarce, while environmental resources such as clean air and water are in many cases severely threatened. It is this combination of limitless individual needs and finite material and environmental resources which sets the stage for a more intensive struggle between individual and societal goals.

This article suggests the direction in which marketing must move in the near future if it is to ameliorate the conflict between individual and societal goals and play a constructive societal role. First, the article considers the present role of marketing in promoting choice. Second, it discusses the traditional relationship between marketing and material consumption. Finally, a course of action is proposed that will help to maintain the future vitality of marketing.

Marketing and consumer choice

In essence, the role of the marketing system is to move goods from producer to consumer. Presumably, in [the USA] the decisions regarding which members of society receive which goods are made through the impersonal force of the 'market mechanism' that allocates scarce resources on the basis of price. In theory, at least, the market mechanism determines the goods to be produced and allocates them on the basis of demand reflected in buyers' willingness to pay. The result is a marketing system which not only moves goods from producer to consumer, but also functions relatively efficiently consistent with market needs.

Marketing and the desire for choice

One basic market need is the desire for choice. The consumer's desire for choice may be latent under conditions of scarcity. However, experience in the U.S. and other nations suggests that this desire manifests itself when the marketing system develops the capacity to generate abundance and to provide a wide variety of goods and services.

As this point is reached, producers and resellers make concerted efforts to discover and satisfy the specific consumer needs which are potentially profitable, and an operating philosophy typified by the term 'marketing concept' begins to emerge. Many products become available in numerous variations, new types of resellers appear, and existing institutions modify their offerings in terms of merchandise, location, and business hours. The net effect is the emergence of a sophisticated marketing system which promotes endless opportunities for choice.

The monetary, or direct, cost of providing the consumer with a wide range of choice, is of necessity, relatively high and is reflected in the price of the products. Both in the U.S. and abroad, increasingly affluent consumers are rejecting the relatively lower costs of standardization and utility and are willing to pay higher prices for greater variety and luxury.

The systems implications of choice

Until very recently, there was no apparent reason to be dissatisfied with this mutually advantageous state of affairs, which resulted in satisfaction for many consumers and in growth and profits for the components of the marketing system. Now, however, there are signs that the marketing system's ability to promote consumption and to provide consumers with a growing range of choice is increasingly inconsistent with the needs of the larger society.

One reason for this is the marketing decisions have been made which expanded the range of consumer product choice but disregarded their environmental impact. There has been a failure to recognize that these products, which are marketing outputs designed for individual satisfaction, are simultaneously inputs to a larger environmental system and as such may affect the well-being of society.

Almost all products have some impact on the environmental system, if not at the point of production, as with food or electric power, then at the point of consumption or disposal. In some cases, these products possess an intrinsic utility that justifies their use regardless of environmental cost. In other instances, the substitution of one product for another reduces adverse environmental effects. For example, the substitution of oil for coal in home heating resulted in the virtual elimination of solid waste disposal in the form of ash.

A problem arises, however, when the individual choice fostered by the marketing system leads to undesirable and unjustifiable societal consequences. For instance, one manifestation of the successful efforts of utilities and appliance manufacturers to promote new uses for electricity has been a major expansion in the sales of residential air conditioners. Between 1964 and 1970, annual sales of window units increased from 2.75 to 5 million, and the household electric bill almost tripled.[3] Yet in fostering this choice for cooling homes over that of natural ventilation or fans, electric utilities and appliance manufacturers have helped to create a situation that poses the broad societal threat of environmental pollution and energy shortage. An additional effect has been the depletion of the nation's reserves of natural gas which currently account for one-sixth of electric power generation. At the present usage rate it is estimated that these reserves will be exhausted in less than ten years.[4]

Other product choices with adverse societal consequences include purchases of detergents versus natural soap products; large cars rather than smaller ones, or public transportation; and the replacement or augmentation of permanent-use products with a plethora of paper and plastic convenience items. The latter items, in particular, are manifestations of a growing trend to product disposability and are contributing to an increase in annual per capita household solid waste generation of approximately 2%.[5] While their consumption is a function of individual purchase choices, the problem of their production and disposal after use is a societal one with direct impact on environmental and material resources. Furthermore, there is no evidence that producers of kitchen garbage disposers have considered their impact on municipal sewage treatment plants, or that producers of power lawn mowers, chain saws, or snow-mobiles have taken account of the cumulative environmental effect of their high level of operating noise.

The net effect of the high level of material consumption of all types engendered by the marketing system is what has been called a 'mass-and-energy nimbus' that, even with fewer people, would threaten the environment.[6]

Defining marketing's responsibility

Under these circumstances, society's situation is analogous to that of a person who buys a beautiful house on a cliff overlooking the sea. Both the view of the sea and the sound of the waves enhance the owner's enjoyment of his property, but each lapping of the waves against the shore subtly undermines the foundations on which the house stands and threatens its ultimate ruin.

In this analogy, marketing's role is that of the seller. As long as the seller is unaware of the future threat to the house and believes that the buyer is receiving what he wants, the seller is morally blameless for subsequent events. But, a heavy moral burden falls upon the seller who knows that the value of what he sells is being systematically undermined.

As this knowledge becomes available, marketing must assume the moral burden. Failure to do so erodes marketing's long-run usefulness to society and implicitly threatens the well-being of individual consumers. Furthermore, the failure to recognize and respond to its responsibility implies that the marketing system will fail to make the adaptation necessary for its healthy survival.

Marketing's pursuit of inappropriate objectives

Emphasis on material consumption

There is no evidence that the marketing system has adjusted its objectives to acknowledge this situation. Those engaged in marketing activities continue to place their primary reliance on the promotion of material consumption. In this regard, their behavior has been consistent with two fundamental values of western society.

The first is the belief that progress is inevitable. In the history of western civilized man, this idea is relatively new and has only appeared in the last two to three hundred years.[7] Nowhere has the belief that conditions will improve with the passage of time been more strongly held than in the United States.

De Toqueville wrote in 1835:

> America is a land of wonders in which everything is in constant motion and every change seems an improvement. The idea of novelty is there indissolubly connected with the idea of amelioration. No natural boundary seems to be set to the efforts of man; and in his eyes what is not yet done is only what he has not yet attempted to do.[8]

A second fundamental western value is that progress can be measured by the growth in material consumption. As Vickers states: 'Whatever else progress may have come to mean, it still means for nearly all of us that collectively at least we should go on consuming progressively more and more ...'[9] This value is reflected in the official concern with the growth in Gross National Product. From the consumer's viewpoint, growth in material consumption is defined as an improvement in the standard of living.

Marketing people have tended to regard this growth as inevitable, and a failure to grow is regarded as a regression rather than as a maintenance of the status quo. Consequently, growth in consumption is perceived to be in complete accord with the prevailing value system, and therefore its appropriateness is not questioned.

However, the current concern with the environment suggests that a value system which regards progress in these terms is no longer compatible with the prevailing conditions in western society, and particularly in the United States. The present U.S. living standard owes much to the nation's resource inventory and the capacity of the environment to assimilate abuse. As the limits of these two factors are reached, society becomes increasingly concerned about the environmentally disadvantageous allocation of resources. Therefore, it should be determined whether the market, or some other method of allocation, should be used to make a rational choice between the acceptance of consumption that results in pollution and the unwillingness to tolerate its effects.[10]

The crux of the problem is that increased material consumption poses a general threat to an environment which may be unable to withstand it even at its present levels. In this sense De Toqueville's 'natural boundary' may have been reached. Through its promotion of this consumption, the present marketing system places an undue strain on both resource inventory and environmental capacity. This is true whether that growth occurs in present markets via increased demand, or in markets created by the development of new products.

The neglect of societal satisfaction

Marketing has also stressed the individual and social satisfactions arising from the purchase and ignored the potential role of societal satisfaction as a purchase incentive. Social satisfaction results from the approval of 'immediate others,' such as family and friends. The source of societal satisfaction is the buyer's knowledge that the purchase benefits the larger society.

Using societal satisfaction as a purchasing criterion, for example, a consumer might derive satisfaction from selecting a laundry detergent which minimizes the water pollution arising from its use. Or a car buyer might not consider those models which are the greatest contributors to the problem of air pollution.

With rare exceptions, the assumption by marketers has been that even if information relating to the societal importance of the purchase is made available the consumer will ignore it. It has been taken for granted that where the opportunities for individual and/or social satisfactions are in conflict with societal considerations, the first two will prevail. Thus, it is assumed that a car buyer will buy a car because he likes it personally (individual satisfaction), or because it will impress his friends (social satisfaction), and that if either or both of these circumstances prevail they will outweigh societal considerations because the benefits of the latter are more remote.

While this may be true, it is essentially a self-fulfilling prophecy. One major reason why societal considerations are not more salient in the purchasing decision is, with minor exceptions, marketer's failure to promote them.

In summary, marketing emphasizes material consumption and ignores considerations of societal benefit when circumstances suggest that this course is no longer suitable. In that sense, the present marketing system is an anachronism.

…

Future alternatives for marketing

The foregoing suggests that marketing decisions will be increasingly shaped by diminishing or limited resources and government intervention. There are several possible responses to this situation. One is to ignore it entirely and to hope that it will disappear with the passage of time. If this approach is taken, most of the decisions fundamental to marketing will be made by the government, possibly in a way which threatens its future as a vital element in society.

A second strategy is to resist any such changes, perhaps through mounting an intensive lobbying effort against legislation that threatens existing marketing practices. This course of action has been followed successfully in the past, especially by large and powerful industry groups. But 'business has not really won or had its way in connection with even a single piece of proposed regulatory or social legislation in the last three quarters of a century ... Sometimes it has taken time to lose, so that at any given time business may have confidently felt itself the victor ...'[11] In the long run, however, the effect is merely a postponement of the inevitable. Change does take place, and while the lobbying industry is sometimes successful in staving off harsh or eccentric provisions in the legislation, the process of resistance can engender public ill-will.

A third approach is acquiescence. Here the companies or industries most affected by impending change are aware of it and are willing to accept it. Thus, unlike the first instance, they are not surprised by legislative action, but passively adjust to the new requirements.

The fourth, and most effective, strategy requires the explicit recognition of the fact that conditions of environmental and material resource stringency inevitably lead to increased government intervention. However, the level of intervention may be minimized if marketers alter their current objective of increasing the material living standard to one which accepts a more stable or reduced level of material consumption.

A major adjustment will be required to change the growth rate in material consumption. Adaptation can be facilitated, however, if the need for the change is anticipated sufficiently early and specific courses of action are actively pursued. These include: (1) Expanding the emphasis on nonmaterial consumption; (2) stressing societal criteria in consumption; and (3) actively participating in formulating the centralized planning policies which affect marketing.

Emphasizing nonmaterial consumption

Companies might adapt to the growing scarcity of resources by shifting their emphasis from the marketing of physical products which consume these resources to the marketing of services. This encompasses both commercial services which benefit individual consumers and firms and social services which directly benefit society.

For example, household cleaning and maintenance services using highly efficient equipment might be lucrative substitute for present marketers of individual household equipment. Apartments with an on-the-premises auto-leasing service would result in the more efficient utilization of automobiles and help alleviate the manifold drain on resources represented by the individual ownership of automobiles. Self-improvement services such as education and vacation activity comprise another area where consumer expenditures involve a relatively small amount of material consumption. These will become increasingly important, since the amount of time spent in a formal work situation is steadily declining.

Another area of opportunity exists in the public sector where the knowledge of the marketing of physical products can be applied to the marketing of such public services as waste disposal and public transportation. Schools, churches, museums, and public libraries can also utilize marketing concepts.[12] This suggests that non-profit organizations would receive benefits from the services of professional marketing agencies similar to those received by industrial clients.

In summary, a basic future thrust of marketing should entail diverting consumers' increasing affluence away from the purchase of material goods and toward the consumption of services.

Stressing societal criteria

To date, societal satisfaction has had either a residual or a negligible influence on consumer purchasing behaviour. However, there are currently numerous indications that societal considerations will assume greater importance as consumers begin to understand the resource implications of product use. This realization is already occurring on a limited scale. For example, in their desire to maintain water quality, some consumers voluntarily witched from phosphate-based detergents to others containing less harmful chemicals.

But, if the quality of the environment is to be protected with minimal government interference, marketers will have to emphasize societal criteria in the promotion of their products. Their long-term objective should be to make societal considerations at least as salient in purchasing behaviour as individual and social gratification. Producers of disposable goods will have to stress the products' ease of disposability to at least the same extent as their use characteristics. Smaller automobiles and automobile substitutes (e.g., rapid transit) will be sold not only on the basis of the dollars they save the consumer, but also on the basis of the economies they represent in terms of air pollution and other resource use that accrue to the entire society.

If effective, this approach would ultimately remove the distinctions between societal and social satisfactions in consumption. Consequently, smaller cars would not be purchased because of societal considerations, but because they had won social acceptance. In contrast, the social stigma would shift to the consumer with big-car preferences.

This may well reinforce a trend which is beginning to appear among the young and which reflects a gradual change in values. There are indications that a growing segment of young American people are rejecting the idea that material consumption is an indication of social worth. This is particularly true in regard to consumption that involves goods associated with some adverse environmental effects. If the trend continues, the ethic of conspicuous consumption that underlies much of contemporary middle-class consumption behaviour will be regarded with the same distaste in the future as today's generation regards the lavish displays of wealth exhibited by the nouveau riche at the turn of the century.

...

The challenge of the future

It may be argued that future technological developments in the fields of recycling, pollution control, and other areas will solve the problems that this article has raised. Undoubtedly, such developments will help to alleviate the problem. However, the countervailing forces of population growth and affluence will continue to aggravate the situation unless additional positive steps are taken.

It has been estimated that by 1985 the average U.S. family will be earning the equivalent of $15,000 in today's purchasing power as compared with $8,600 in 1969. Population growth will account for approximately 30% of the growth in terms of increased expenditures for housing, transportation, and recreation. The remaining 70% will result from affluence and will be manifested by a greater demand for more luxurious goods and services.[13]

Marketing will help determine the extent to which this affluence is channelled into either materialistic consumption or amenities and services. A continuation of the present stress on the former will result in individual short-term benefits, but may ultimately strain the resources of society, perhaps to the breaking point. On the other hand, by shifting the emphasis to nonmaterial consumption and societal considerations marketing will be acting on the long-run interests of society and will be facilitating the preservation of its future freedom of action. This is the nature of the challenge facing marketing.

(Source: Feldman, L. P., 1971, 'Societal adaptation: a new challenge for marketing', Journal of Marketing, Vol. 35, No. 3, pp. 54–60.)

End notes

[1] William Lazer, 'Marketing's Changing Social Relationships,' *Journal of Marketing*, Vol. 33 (January, 1969), pp. 3–9, at p. 8.

[2] Leslie M. Dawson, 'The Human Concept: New Philosophy for Business,' *Business Horizons*, Vol. XII (December, 1969), pp. 29–38.

[3] 'Electric Power Demands Clash with Environmental Needs,' *Congressional Quarterly Weekly Report*, Vol. 28 (May 1, 1970), pp. 1175–1178, at p. 1175.

[4] Same reference as footnote 3 p. 1176. …

[5] Blair T. Bower, et al., *Water Management* (New York: Regional Plan Association, 1968), p. 46.

[6] Max Ways, 'How to Think About the Environment,' *Fortune*, Vol. LXXXI (February, 1970), pp. 98–191 ff., at p. 101.

[7] Sir Geoffrey Vickers, *Value Systems and Social Processes* (Toronto, Canada: Tavistock Publications, 1968), p. 6.

[8] Alexis de Toqueville *Democracy in America,* Part I (New York: Alfred A. Knopf, Inc., 1945), Chapter 18.

[9] Same reference as footnote 7, p. 15.

[10] Robert U. Ayres and Allen V. Kneese, 'Production, Consumption and Externalities,' *American Economic Review,* Vol. LIX (June, 1969), pp. 282–297, at p. 293.

[11] Theodore Levitt, 'Why Business Always Loses,' *Harvard Business Review*, Vol. 46 (March–April, 1968), pp. 81–99, at p. 82.

[12] Philip Kotler and Sidney J. Levy, 'Broadening the Concept of Marketing,' *Journal of Marketing*, Vol. 33 (January, 1969), pp. 10–15.

[13] Herman P. Miller, 'Is Overpopulation Really the Problem,' *Conference Board RECORD*, Vol. VII (May, 1970), pp. 19–22, at pp. 21–22.

Acknowledgements

Grateful acknowledgement is made to the following sources for permission to reproduce material in this book:

Text

Example 3.1: Osborne, H., 'Endowment firm fined £750,000', *Guardian*, January 12, 2006, Reproduced with permission of Guardian Newspaper Limited; *Essential Reading 1:* Levitt, T., 'Marketing Myopia', © 1960 by the President and Fellows of Harvard College. All Rights Reserved. Further copying without permission of Harvard Business School is prohibited. *Essential Reading 2*: Porter, M. E., 'How competitive forces shape strategy' © 1979 by the President and Fellows of Harvard College. All Rights Reserved. Further copying without permission of Harvard Business School is prohibited. *Essential Reading 3*: Crane, A. and Matten, D. (2003) Chapter 8: 'Consumer and Business Ethics' from *Business Ethics*. By permission of Oxford University Press; *Essential Reading 4*: Feldman, L. P. 'Societal adaptation: a new challenge for marketing', *Journal of Marketing,* Vol. 35, No. 3, July 1971, American Marketing Association.

Figures

Figures 2.1, 4.3 and 4.4: Blythe, J. (2005) *Essentials of Marketing,* Pearson Education Limited © Pearson Education Limited 2001, 2005; *Figure 3.1:* from Kotler, P. et al. (2001) *Principles of Marketing*, Pearson Education Limited © Pearson Education Limited 2001; *Figure 3.2:* adapted from Henry Assael, (1987) *Consumer Behaviour and Marketing Action*, 6th edn, p. 67, Boston, MA, Kent Publishing Company © Wadsworth Inc. 1987; *Figures 3.3, 4.1 and 4.2*: Kotler, P. et al. (2001) *Principles of Marketing*, Pearson Education Limited © Pearson Education Limited 2001; *Figure 5.1:* Kotler, P. (1972) 'What consumerism means for markets', *Harvard Business Review*, May–June © 1972 by the President and Fellows of Harvard College. All Rights Reserved.

Photographs/Illustrations

Page 7: Scott Masear/CartoonStock Ltd; *Page 10:* © Jim Sizemore/ CartoonStock Ltd; *Page 14:* © AMET JEAN PIERRE/CORBIS SYGMA; *Page 20:* © Purestock/Alamy; *Page 25*: © Royalty-Free/Corbis; *Page 29:* © Paul Souders/Corbis; *Pages 36, 39 and 67*: © John Morris/CartoonStock Ltd; *Page 41*: © Hulton-Deutsch Collection/CORBIS; *Page 54:* © Photofusion Picture Library/Alamy; *Page 66:* © fStop/Alamy.

Cover

© Royalty free/Corbis.

Module team

B120 team

Dr Anja Schaefer
Dr Nik Winchester
Dr Warren Smith
Dr Vira Krakhmal
Barry Jones, *Curriculum Manager*
Carey Stephens
Susan Hughes
Rosie McGookin
Val O'Connor, *Curriculum Assistant*

The original course team

Dr Diane Preston, *Course Team Chair*
Patricia McCarthy, *Course Manager*
Dr Kirstie Ball
Penny Marrington
Fran Myers
Dr Anja Schaefer
Dr George Watson
Rita Gregory, *Course Team Assistant*
Val O'Connor, *Course Team Assistant*

Other contributors

Dr Lorna J. Eller
Mick Fryer
Jonathan Winship

External examiner

Kate Greenan, *Professor of Management Education and Head of School of Accounting, Ulster University*

Developmental testers

Linda Fisher
Adam Messer
John Messer
Marina Ramtohul

Critical readers

Patricia Coffey, *Senior Lecturer, University of Brighton Business School*
Clare Cromarty, *OUBS Associate Lecturer*
Patricia Dawson, *Principal Lecturer, Thames Valley University, retired*
Helen Higson, *Director of Undergraduate Studies, Aston Business School*

Beverly Leeds, *Principal Lecturer, University of Central Lancashire*
Nigel Walton, *OUBS Associate Lecturer*

The production team

Martin Brazier, *Graphic Designer*
Angela Davies, *Media Assistant*
Richard Dobson, *Editor*
Hannah Eiseman-Renyard, *Editor*
Diane Hopwood, *Rights Assistant*
Lee Johnson, *Media Project Manager*
Siggy Martin, *Assistant Print Buyer*
Katy Nyaaba, *Media Assistant*
Jill Somerscales, *Editor*

The original production team

Holly Clements, *Media Assistant*
Lene Connolly, *Print Buyer*
Jonathan Davies, *Graphic Designer*
Julie Fletcher, *Media Project Manager*
Fiona Harris, *Editor*
Diane Hopwood, *Compositor*
Kate Hunter, *Editor*
Jon Owen, *Graphic Artist*
Deana Plummer, *Picture Researcher*
Nikki Smith, *Assistant Print Buyer*
Jill Somerscales, *Editor*